MODERN
Cape Malay
COOKING

COMFORT FOOD INSPIRED BY
MY CAPE MALAY HERITAGE

CARIEMA ISAACS

I am so proud of Cariema for once again choosing to honour and celebrate the wonderful Cape Malay cuisine that we all love and enjoy, and for continuing the tradition of passing down food memories through these amazing recipes. This is how culture and heritage are preserved and kept alive! Well done! I wish you every success and I can't wait for everyone to have this amazing book in their kitchens.

All my love, Mogau

Mogau Seshoene, "The Lazy Makoti"

Cariema's food is spoken in a language rich with emotions, memories and traditions. Every dish is an expression of love and caring. Cooking becomes a deep conversation of life and loss, of longing and joy. Her latest collection of recipes speaks clearly in her mother tongue with an inborn generosity and understanding of both the fundamentals of cooking and the building blocks of flavours. There are no secrets, she reveals it all, from how to cook in the morning light to deciphering the perfect Gatsby.

Modern Cape Malay Cooking is a book to devour from start to finish, each chapter a fusion of her Cape Malay roots and her own discoveries of other cultures and faraway cuisines. She brings a modern mindset to comforting food from the past, draws inspiration from her wealth of food friendships and makes us all part of her inner circle and family.

Errieda du Toit
Food culture commentator

What more can be said for the Cape Malay home cook and chef, Cariema Isaacs, who knows her way around the kitchen and our tastebuds? It's very lekker to know you, and I am inspired by the strides you have taken on this journey in honouring and celebrating your heritage and the lives of those most near and dear to you.

Marc Jacobs
Co-founder of Vannie Kaap

Beautifully written and filled with love, this book is for everyone who has lost someone but feels their presence through the power of food. Like any Cape Malay cook worth her salt, Cariema has effortlessly packed a love-filled cookbook with flavour, memory and beautifully developed recipes that leaves one salivating at the thought of cooking them.

Fatima Saib
Multimedia Commercial Editor for *Woolworths TASTE*, content creator, podcaster

This is simply a pure gold collection of Cape Malay recipes – a mix of traditional and more up-to-date dishes. Cariema knows how to create unpretentious but absolutely delicious food that everyone would love – spicy, saucy and packed with flavour!

Daleen van der Merwe
Lifestyle and digital content creator

Dedication

For my mom,
the quintessential Cape Malay domestic goddess
1 August 1949–30 August 2021

There are losses that rearrange the world.
Deaths that change the way you see everything,
grief that tears everything down.
Pain that transports you to an entirely different universe...

Megan Devine, *It's OK That You're Not OK*

Published in 2023 by Penguin Books,
    an imprint of Penguin Random House
    South Africa (Pty) Ltd
Company Reg. No. 1953/000441/07
The Estuaries, 4 Oxbow Crescent,
    Century Avenue, Century City, 7441
PO Box 1144, Cape Town, 8000, South Africa

www.penguinrandomhouse.co.za

ISBN 978-1-48590-145-7

PUBLISHER: Beverley Dodd
MANAGING EDITOR: Aimee Carelse
EDITOR: Joy Nel
DESIGNER: Randall Watson
PROOFREADER & INDEXER: Cecilia Barfield
PHOTOGRAPHER: Turhaan Samodien
FOOD STYLIST: Cariema Isaacs
STYLIST'S ASSISTANT: Lani Aragon

Reproduction: Studio Repro
Printed and bound in China by 1010
    Printing International Ltd.

CONTENTS

Foreword by Farzana Kumandan

Founder of food blog Sprinkles and Spice;
Food Editor for 'The Voice'

Bismillah-ir-Rahman-ir-Rahim
'In the Name of God, Most Merciful, Most Compassionate'

Cooking is an integral part of who I am. It's etched deep inside me – it's my happy place, my de-stress, my therapy and one of the ways I show love. It's around a wholesome meal, amid the chitter and chatter of our loved ones, where sublime food memories are made – this is love and feasting in action.

Every new endeavour is started with the Arabic salutation of 'Bismillah', as I have done here at the start of this foreword, and it's no different when it comes to cooking and baking. This salutation is associated with what Muslims call 'barakah' (blessings). Essentially, we call on God to bless the food we are going to cook and, in doing so, it allows us to share that blessing with those near and dear to us. Any celebratory feast or social event, such as a wedding or even a thikr (prayer gathering), is concluded with the barakah of sharing a meal together. An incomparable bond binds us together, whether it is one person cooking or everyone bringing along something for us all to share – it's an innate sense of love, family and community.

Our senses are our guides – a meal can conjure up food nostalgia from our childhood, and an aroma can spur on a trip down memory lane. For me, it is the aromatics, the spices and the fragrances thereof, that take me back to where my own food journey began. As a little girl, I would spend hours in the kitchen watching my mom and both my grannies – my Daadi (paternal grandmother) and Naani (maternal grandmother) – creating dish upon dish with nothing short of love and culinary passion.

Every meal began with the preparation of spices. Both my grandmothers were born in India and, to them, buying ground or powdered spices was sacrilegious. Instead, they would purchase whole spices in their purest form, sometimes still in the husk. As a little girl I watched these spices being prepared, sun-dried, often toasted or roasted and then, finally, being ground and blended to form a fine powder or paste. The fragrances were mesmerising, finding their way into every part of our home, and my grandmothers, with their golden and crimson spice-stained fingertips, would create the most flavoursome biryanis and aromatic aknis, spicy curries and even spicier atchars!

Every dish spoke of love and every flavour profile was an insight into a life lived in celebration of food. Yet no recipe was used – it was all down to skill and experience, naturally cultivated from what they were taught in *their* mothers' kitchens. As a teen, I found myself documenting everything from ingredients to method, eventually accumulating a compilation of treasured recipes and cherished memories.

As time went by, my compilations of tattered, spice-stained pages and dishevelled journals became an ensemble of valuable food memories, as I would recollect not only the dishes, but also the time spent in my families' kitchens. These recipes are like a time capsule now and as much as they transport me back to the past, they also centre me in my own home kitchen. These days I cook with the knowledge that I have my grandmothers with me. It is for this reason that I find recipes, especially handwritten ones, enthralling.

This brings me to my dearest Cariema, someone I was blessed enough to meet during my foodie journey. Cariema is a selfless soul with a huge heart, willing to help and share her knowledge with everyone. Her warmth, kindness, enthusiasm and zest for life is a force like no other and you never walk away from a conversation with her without feeling inspired. Her cookbooks are compilations of recipes, a celebration of food, feasting, friends and family.

Every one of her recipes tells a story and every story provides insight into her Cape Malay heritage, her personal journey and her travels – regardless of where she goes, she takes all of us along with her.

This cookbook, *Modern Cape Malay Cooking*, is Cariema personified – you will find nuances of her and her heritage as you turn the pages, her vibrancy comes through the images and her heart-print is delicately woven into her writing. This cookbook has a bit of everything: a beautiful story, a celebration of family, friends and culture, and the fundamentals of Halaal and Cape Malay cooking.

It is clear through all our conversations, Cariema's social media posts and her cookbooks that Cape Town remains her home regardless of where she finds herself in the world – for her, home truly is where the heart is. Compiled from countless memories and dedicated to her late mother, it goes without saying that Cariema has her mom and her whole heart in this book. Her mother's legacy continues to live on through her, and so another Cape Malay domestic goddess is born.

Foreword by Ingrid Jones

Co-founder of Mikateko Media and The Lockdown Recipe Facebook Group, curator of *The Lockdown Recipe Storytelling Book*, television personality and food culture commentator

I'm the descendant of a Christian father and a Muslim mother – in relation to food language, that already reverberates of two food cultures in one home. My mom fused into my father's family's way of cooking. This meant that curries (yellow, sweet and sour) were adopted and adapted to appeal to our Christian family's palate and household, and these curries were traditionally served for Sunday lunch.

In my teenage years, more specifically when I turned 13, I was bundled off to boarding school, since we were living in a small town with no established secondary or high school and miles away from family. This move allowed me to be closer to my mom's Muslim family and on the days that we were allowed to leave the boarding school (Wednesdays and weekends), I would make a beeline to the homes of the family I was getting to know better. These visits incorporated conversation, connection and a new culinary adventure in the form of spicy meals, plates of samoosas and daltjies, fragrant biryanis and rosewater-infused boeber. This was my rite of passage

into Cape Malay dishes. Words like jeera (cumin) and dhania (coriander), cardamon and cinnamon became part of my vocabulary, and these spices became the warmth of a love language spoken between me and my family.

Years later, when I relocated to Cape Town to attend university, another gastronomic adventure awaited, and my palate was exposed to much more than just spicy curries. I'd make my way to my best friend Abeedah Dollie's home – truth be told, her dad nearly barred me from visiting because I'd show up at dinner time almost every night. Abeedah's mom, Mrs Dollie, was my window into the more traditional Cape Malay cooking and cuisine. Her repertoire of dishes extended beyond the biryanis, curries and samoosas I was accustomed to. It is in her kitchen that I learned about denningvleis, mavrou, masala chops, delicious desserts and many, many more Cape Malay delicacies.

In 2020, at the height of the Covid-19 pandemic, I decided to start a foodie group on Facebook called the Lockdown Recipe Storytelling Group, which eventually translated into the *Lockdown Recipe Storytelling Cookbook*. It is in this group where I met the beautiful Cariema Isaacs, before having an opportunity to meet her in person, after she initiated contact with me via social media. I was overawed to say the least. She was, in every sense, so much more than what I had anticipated – and how did she even know that I existed? Well, the rest as they say is history! Through her and so many other Cape Malay home cooks and chefs, I have learnt about the fine art of presenting your culture on a plate. It's through Cariema that I value my mom's contribution to my own food journey, all intertwined with my appreciation and love of life.

South Africa has a multitude of food komvandaan (where we come from) stories, each unique and colourful, vivid and meaningful. Cariema Isaacs' Cape Malay storytelling assists in the depiction of the history and heritage of Cape Malay cuisine, and the role that every tietie, aunty, boeta and uncle has played shaping our experience with food.

Introduction

Terima Kasih – Tramakasie
(Thank you)

'... the love language of the Cape Malays is FOOD'

'Terima Kasih' is the Indonesian expression for thank you, passed on by our forebears and therefore still part of the Cape Malay vernacular. It is spelt slightly differently in South Africa (tramakasie) and pronounced as 'tram-ma-kas-see', which incidentally is used *only* by Cape Malays in Cape Town. This expression of thanks defines the Cape Malay demeanor and the gratitude we feel for what we have in our lives, who we have in our lives and ultimately for the life we have been granted. Our thankfulness is also expressed through food. We do not know how to cook without giving thanks to God for the ingredients that grace our kitchens and, though we love to eat, we become somewhat morose when we must eat alone. Therefore, most meals in Cape Malay homes are served at the table and most seats are never empty.

I found myself smack in the middle of the Covid-19 pandemic while writing the manuscript for this book, where travelling home to Cape Town had become vastly challenging and the longing for family, friends and home food intensified. The only thing that could diminish the ache I felt during this time was cooking, or writing, and since I am deeply drawn to both, the manuscript for *Modern Cape Malay Cooking* unfolded.

This cookbook is a celebration of food and feasting, and provides a contemporary view of Cape Malay cuisine and the simplicity of home cooking. There is nothing more indulgent than the aromas of morsels of garlic and sliced onions or potatoes, cosying up to a drizzle of warm oil and melted butter – simple ingredients and vibrant aromatics in the hands of anyone who is curious and courageous enough to create flavour!

The recipes in this cookbook define Cape Malay home cooking and showcase a fusion of flavours that redefined the modern Cape Malay palate. Though traditional Cape Malay cuisine and recipes have stood the test of time, there have also been adaptations that have given rise to a culinary fusion. These adaptations could be anything from what the Cape Malay millennial generation crave these days, or the substitution of ingredients to accommodate health and dietary needs, to the culinary influences that richly contributed to the Cape Malay palate over time. The younger Cape Malay generation yearned for more of the popular dishes from the East and West, a comforting pasta or quick-and-easy stir-fry – but with a Cape Malay twist. By 'twist' I mean it must be spicy, it must be saucy and it must be packed with flavour!

The new generation also brought with it a flurry of food bloggers who continue to inspire our culinary fare by telling their stories of food and heritage, depicted through vivid photography and sophisticated food styling. Also, since most Cape Malays follow the Islamic faith, it's also essential to understand the sacred context behind the preparation of our dishes. The customisation, for instance, of a Mexican Chilli Con Carne, Mongolian Beef, or an Italian Risotto, where pork and alcohol are omitted, is to ensure that the religious dietary requirements are met in the context of Halaal ingredients and cooking.

I would also like to dispel this foolish notion that Cape Malay cooking is free-form (the ideology that measurements are not used), and that we call on our ancestors to tell us when to stop adding a pinch of this and a spoonful of that – it is horribly inaccurate. My grandmother taught me to measure when cooking and baking, and that consistency is key; this way a recipe is preserved in its purest form.

Lastly, the Cape Malays' generosity of spirit remains ever present and is reminiscent of our community, as we share our food regardless of how little we may have. Maybe this is also the reason why our dishes are never prepared as a single serving – we'd like to believe that if an unexpected visitor arrived we would be able to offer them a warm meal.

Monisha Bharadwaj, who wrote *The Indian Cookery Course*, said: 'Food is central to an Indian person's life. It is spoken about all the time, is a great icebreaker and is cooked and eaten throughout the day. The highest demonstration of love in India is to feed someone.'

I share the same sentiment about my Cape Malay community and our culinary ideology. Our homes welcome anyone who steps over our threshold, and even if we have not prepared a meal, then a warm cup of tea becomes an invitation for our visitors to stay. Once they stay, it wouldn't be too long before a steady conversation starts flowing and a heartfelt connection is fostered. There are even times when a disagreement is settled over food, in the hopes of finding our peace and balance with the other person again.

Suffice to say that the love language of the Cape Malays is FOOD, and I say 'tramakasie' every day that I get to express myself in this way.

Cariema Isaacs
Dubai, 2022

Family Tree

To me, the Hartleys were and still are the quintessential master chefs of Cape Malay home cooking and baking!

RAGHMAH HARTLEY ISAACS – my Ouma taught me *how* to cook

I spent most of my childhood in my grandmother's kitchen in Bo-Kaap, the Cape Malay Quarter in Cape Town, South Africa. This is where my love for cooking, baking and our Cape Malay culinary heritage began. For many years to come, I would learn how to cook and bake traditional Cape Malay fare as my grandmother took me under her wing. She, Raghmah Hartley, was to me the embodiment of a Cape Malay cook. She was also surrounded by master chefs, from her brother Omar Hartley to her sisters (who I knew as Aunty Aysa, Aunty Hajira and Aunty Mariam), all phenomenal home cooks and bakers. Their culinary prowess was cultivated by their mother, my great-grandmother Amiena Hartley, who was known as Memmer in our family circles. My father had so many food tales to tell about Memmer's cooking and baking, which included our traditional Cape Malay fare: koolfrikkadelle; penslawer; pienang curry, pootjies in tamatie, sweet yellow rice with raisins and coconut, Eid fruitcake and old-fashioned tray bakes, as well as jam and coconut tarts.

My Bo-Kaap Ouma could cook a meal in no time, without fuss or frenzy. She preferred to use fresh ingredients; therefore meat, fish, poultry and vegetables were purchased on the same day and never refrigerated or frozen for long periods of time. Spices were purchased in small amounts from the local spice trader, and decanted and stored in glass jars. If the appearance and aroma of the spices seemed dull and bland, she'd discard and replace them with fresh spices. I have so many sweet memories of her home kitchen, where I learnt the art of Cape Malay cooking and baking. It's no coincidence that our first culinary teachers are our mother and grandmothers, and it personally remains a beacon that vibrates through the heart of my home, my kitchen.

MOEGAMAD RASHAAD ISAACS – my father taught my *why* we cook

My grandmother might have taught me how to cook, but what I learnt from my father was even more valuable: the comprehension of why we cook. Cooking, in his view, was a form of meditation or prayer, as it is for most Cape Malay cooks. He couldn't enter into cooking without giving thanks to God first, for providing sustenance to his family. My father viewed food as he did love; he believed that it was what the human body and soul needed to feel nourished. He was convinced that through food, he shared a part of who he was with those near and dear to him. Therefore, many of the dishes and meals he cooked would be shared and guests were always welcomed at our table. My father's creed was this: 'If you are going to cook, you must cook with love. And if you are going to eat, you must eat with someone, never alone.'

MY MOM'S SIDE OF THE FAMILY –

From the Lagardien legacy to the Solomon poise,
our family's Cape Malay domestic goddesses were born!

ZAINAB LAGARDIEN SOLOMON – my Big Ma taught me how to become a phenomenal woman!
From her cookbook, *Traditional Cape Malay Cooking*:

'I was born at no. 14 Godfrey Street, off Hanover Street in District Six. I was only six years old when my mother and the baby were laid to rest, and I went to live with my grandmother. She was a well-known konfyt-maker, catering for special functions, and her life was a colourful one. She reared us on home-made breads and konfyts, so the introductions to cooking for me and my sister began at an early age.'

My Big Ma was one of the most unconventional and eccentric women I knew and, from her, I learnt how to dream and how to dream BIG! She was flamboyant and sassy, and her zest for life rubbed off on me at a very early age. My grandmother ventured into the kitchens of the Clarendon Hotel in Cape Town, was featured in the local newspapers for her recipe submissions and eventually ended up writing cookbooks. She was adventurous when it came to cooking and baking, and experimented with soya as a substitute for meat – when very few Cape Malay cooks would – thereby transforming some traditional, meat-based Cape Malay dishes into vegan- and vegetarian-friendly ones. My grandmother hosted luncheons and dinner parties, and the place settings would be every bit as glamorous as she was. I am therefore honoured that I could use her handwritten recipes in this cookbook. Big Ma, "I carry your heart with me (I carry it in my heart)".

RASHIEDAH SOLOMON ISAACS – my mom taught me how to become a domestic goddess

My mom's poise and femininity were reflected in all the elements that encompassed her domestic goddess persona. From the way she cooked and baked, to the way she spoke, to the way she set the table and how she juggled a career.

I never knew just how much I had been influenced by my mother until she passed away in August 2021. My mom did it all: she had a career while raising three kids and managed a demanding household. I don't remember a weekend at my parents' home without guests, friends or family popping by for a warm meal or a comforting cup of tea.

There are so many memories I have of my mom, but one of my fondest is of her on Eid morning. I'd watch her at 5 a.m., rolling out layers of flaky pastry that she had prepared the day before. She'd spoon a peppery steak and kidney filling into a pastry-lined pie dish, ready to be baked for Eid breakfast. I'd observe her place a pristine white tablecloth on the table and then, like a well-choreographed dance, she'd start placing decorative bowls, shiny cutlery and ornate cake plates on the table. I'd be frolicking about in my PJs, with tousled hair, filling the bowls with sweets and chocolates.

Years later, I'd witness my mom struggle with anxiety and depression and eventually dementia. One of her most traumatic depressive episodes occurred when I was about 12 years old. It was also at this time that I had to take on more responsibilities at home, more specifically in the kitchen. Though it might have seemed like a daunting task at the time, I realise now that it was my rite of passage into our home kitchen – for the first time, I was cooking and baking without supervision. The mantle had been passed on to me and whether it was the Eid table being set or just a Sunday lunch being prepared, another domestic goddess was born!

BACK TO BASICS

THE FUNDAMENTALS OF
CAPE MALAY-INSPIRED CUISINE

This chapter provides insight into the fundamental principles that define the Cape Malay culinary ethos. It also symbolises a heartfelt welcome into my home kitchen, which for most Cape Malays remains the heart of the home. The energy that exists in my home kitchen brings calm to chaotic days and postulates peaceful equilibrium – within seconds a space filled with spices, ingredients and kitchen essentials transforms into a comforting sanctuary. This is where I find my bliss, with an attuned consciousness of this space, and where I am instantly connected to my heritage.

Cape Malays are known to be brilliant storytellers and our experiences and memories of cooking, feasting and baking with our friends and family remain the most cherished recollections of home. These days our stories are told via bloggers and social media influencers, food writers and chefs, vlogs and YouTube channels. The age of social media and technology has allowed our food stories to enter homes of people who never knew what Cape Malay cooking was. The more curious people became, the more stories were being shared and soon food conversations connected us all to one another – suffice to say, we ended up *virtually* breaking bread together.

The food blog and television show *CookHalaal* was created by sisters Gadija Gamieldien and Mymoena Bey back in 2017. They describe their blog as a culinary destination featuring a curated selection of Halaal-compliant recipes with contributors from around the globe. Gadija and I got on like a house on fire. We couldn't stop talking about our heritage and what Cape Malay food meant to us, and this fortified our newfound kinship. *CookHalaal* had a vision to share food stories long before the Covid-19 pandemic drew most of us back into our kitchens. The culinary talent of Cape Malay and Halaal cooks was celebrated further with their *CookHalaal* website and other social media platforms. For the first time, the spotlight was being shone on Halaal food, which brings me to the significance of this first chapter of the book. To gain greater insight into Cape Malay cuisine, you must understand that religion and religious dietary requirements largely influence the Cape Malay culinary creed and palate.

The religious context to Halaal cooking and eating

'Halaal' is an Arabic word that means lawful or permissible, and commonly refers to what's allowed under Islamic law. When it comes to food and drink, the concept of Halaal is like that of kosher in Judaism. Non-muslims often think that in order for a dish to be Halaal it should not contain pork and/or alcohol. The fact is, Halaal food extends beyond the exclusion of pork and alcohol. Halaal food preparation, for instance, is largely determined by how the animal was slaughtered and/or whether it died of an illness or natural causes.

For meat to be certified Halaal, it must be slaughtered in a manner where the jugular vein, carotid artery and windpipe are cut in one swift motion, with a sharp knife, without allowing the animal to suffer. The same process also allows all blood to drain from the carcass, since the consumption of blood is considered prohibited in Islam.

The most fundamental act during the slaughtering process is that a prayer is recited, which is also known as the Shahada. This is an act of worship that is also a reminder to all Muslims that the slaughter of the animal is not done in vain since the meat will be used to feed families, and ultimately sustain and nourish the body.

To further elaborate, Muslims believe that Halaal food brings with it some benefit to one's body versus the risk that non-Halaal food poses. Therefore, the following types of meat are not Halaal, regardless of its preparation:

- Pork and any of its by-products
- Reptiles
- Birds of prey
- Horses, donkeys, mules
- Fanged animals, i.e. dogs, cats
- Some other animals, such as monkeys

Alcohol

Alcohol and all intoxicants are considered haram (forbidden) to Muslims. Therefore, Cape Malays do not consume alcohol, whether it be in liquid form or added to cooking or baking.

The Cape Malay kitchen

The culinary culture of the Cape Malays has been influenced by British and Dutch cuisine, but largely by the cuisines of Malaysia and Indonesia, the regions where our forebears come from. Additionally, the Indian influence in the Cape Malay culture is attributed to the generations of intermarriage and union between the Cape Malay and Muslim-Indian communities in South Africa. Therefore meat, fish, chicken and rice are staples, and there is strong emphasis on spices and herbs, such as ginger, garlic, chillies, curry leaves and coriander. A Cape Malay meal is incomplete without a cooling or spicy condiment, and it's almost mandatory to have a sweet and tangy blatjang or chutney served with grilled fish or a roast. It goes without saying that the Cape Malay menu places serious emphasis on the main meal and the condiments that complement it. Appetisers and desserts are often seen as a bonus, because even a cup of tea after dinner is sufficient to end off a meal.

Different cuts of meat used for Cape Malay cooking

The rule of thumb is that for most stew-like or curried dishes, shoulder or leg of lamb would be used – always cubed or cut into bite-size portions, and always with the bone in.

Bredies

A bredie is like a hearty stew, slow-cooked and loaded with vegetables or pulses or legumes. Shoulder or leg of lamb is most often used, as described above, although beef has become a substitute since lamb has become more expensive. Cubed beef is often used, but beef with the bone in, such as beef shin and blade beef, are preferred for depth of flavour.

Stocks

Traditional Cape Malay cooking does not make use of stocks, very much like Indian cooking. The base of most Cape Malay dishes includes finely chopped onions, garlic and green chilli that would have been sautéed in a drizzle of oil, and then lightly braised or browned. A dash of water is added every now and again to stop the onions from sticking. At the same time, the caramelisation of the onions and garlic creates further depth of flavour, and is an essential step for most traditional Cape Malay dishes. For dishes where a saucy base is needed, finely chopped tomato would be added to the onions, garlic and chilli. It is then slow-cooked until all the ingredients have rendered and a lush sauce is formed. A dash or two of granulated sugar is added to create a perfect balance of sweet and sour. The base sauce is also doused with small amounts of water, which often also determines how liquified your base sauce will be.

Bones

The only time you'll notice bones being removed from cuts of meat will be when a lamb or beef curry is being prepared and used as a filling for a salomie (flat bread or wrap filled with curry). A Cape Malay home cook views the bones, and more importantly, the marrow of the bones, to be the epitome of flavour! The nuttiness of the marrow creates depth of flavour that is perfect for slow-cooked dishes. This is also why our soups are often meat-based because traditionally all Cape Malay soups contained beef marrow bones. The flavour is thus derived this way instead of using a stock.

Tomato and Onion Relish
(page 189)

Roasted Beetroot and
Onion Salad (page 190)

Zahra's Zesty Brinjal
Atchar (page 188)

Malaysian Sweet
Chilli Sambal
(Page 193)

Seasoning

I don't know any Cape Malay home kitchen that doesn't have a well-stocked spice drawer, cupboard or pantry! We are also not averse to trying new spice pastes or seasonings. A hit of heat awakes the senses, but we don't like blistering hot spice concoctions. It's also fair to say that if a Cape Malay cook had only salt and pepper at their disposal, these would be enough to season a meal. Therefore, most of our traditional bredies are lightly seasoned with salt and pepper and, for some, a hint of nutmeg or dried chilli flakes or whole spices like allspice and/or cloves are added.

Roasts, curries and grills

The essence of Cape Malay cuisine is largely influenced by our ancestors hailing from Indonesia and Malaysia. To understand this a little better, you need to go a step further by exploring these two cuisines individually.

Indonesian cuisine is extremely diverse but largely indigenous to the surrounding islands, without outside influence apart from some Dutch colonial influences.

Malaysian cuisine on the other hand has been largely shaped by the strong influences from China and India. This explains the Cape Malays' love for curries, spices and accompanying condiments. Furthermore, our affinity for roasting and grilling are amplified by our South African braai culture. A glorious union develops where the gentle heat of warm coals entices the Cape Malay cook to marinate sosaties, kebabs and chops, ultimately to partake in the age-old tradition of 'open fire' cooking. The marinades are bold in colour, rich in taste and have a distinctive sweet and sour flavour profile – all reminiscent of our Asian roots.

The technique taught to me by my Bo-Kaap Ouma

The two most significant lessons I was taught by my Ouma when cooking are as follows: don't rush the process, and listen to the sounds of the ingredients when they are cooking. When you're braising onions or meat, listen for a soft sizzle, one that's slightly muffled – this is an indication that you will need to add a dash of water to the pot just before the sizzle becomes more and more prominent. By a dash of water, she meant no more than a quarter cup. Anything more will mean that you will be required to reduce the sauce again; this can also give the meat a lacklustre colour while searing it. When the water has been added, give the pot or pan a good shake and reduce the heat. Allow the ingredients to simmer ever so gently until you hear that dull sizzle again, then add another dash of water. This technique creates the browning or braising that is reminiscent of a Cape Malay bredie that is known as a 'smoor'.

The concept of 'lang sous' (saucy, gravy-based dishes)

The concept of having a gravy-like sauce for most dishes is because most traditional Cape Malay dishes are also served with rice, and therefore the sauce is ideal to complement the starch. The gravy also increases the quantity of the meal, thus more people can be fed. This is why 'lang sous' meals are often served at larger festivities or occasions, such as weddings or funerals, Eid lunches and so on.

The Cape Malay curry sauce and the significance of the appearance

Cape Malays pride themselves on their curries, and the complexion of the sauce is often an indicator of how scrumptious the curry will be. The rule of thumb is that the sauce should be brightly coloured, tinged with turmeric to create that fresh, yellow appearance, as opposed to a dull terracotta-like colour resembling a stew. The latter is often an indication that the onions or some of the ingredients have been slightly burned or overcooked.

A Cape Malay curry sauce's essence is that perfect balance of sweet and sour. A good amount of freshly grated tomato is added to create the lush curry sauce, often complemented by either a hint of tomato paste or canned tomatoes. Granulated white sugar rounds off the sauce, leaving a hint of sweetness on the tastebuds. Finally, a curry sauce must contain garlic, ginger, green chillies, curry leaves, fresh coriander leaves and a medley of curry spices such as turmeric, ground cumin and a blended masala. Curry powders were very popular in the past, but since there are so many blended masala powders to choose from today, most curries often contain a leaf masala, kokni masala, roasted masala, meat masala, seafood masala, and so on – the list is endless!

A curry is often complemented by the starch or grain it is served with

I'll start by saying that for most Cape Malay meat-based curries, potatoes are essential, and the slow cooking of these potatoes also creates depth of flavour. Perfection is associated with the tenderness not only of the meat, but also of the potatoes. The complementing starch or grain that accompanies a curry dish is usually a feathery light jasmine or basmati rice, and/or a traditional Cape Malay flaky roti. The idea is to mop up the curry sauce with the starch, feathery light potatoes and tender cuts of meat, infused with aromatics and almost squished together to create a little portion of perfection before it's devoured. However, these days a multitude of other grains like quinoa, freekeh, couscous and bulgur have become heathier substitutes in relation to the starches.

The secret code

Cape Malay cooking may not be a science, but like most traditional and heritage cuisines it has history, technique and culinary prowess that has been handed down from one generation of cooks to another. It's for this reason that most of the authentic recipes and dishes are best when sampled in the homes of the older generation of Cape Malay cooks rather than in restaurants, take-away shops or cafés. They still cook with what I believe is the secret code, the same code that was handed down from my great-grandmothers to my Big Ma and Ouma, to my Pappa and mom and then to me.

The secret code has very little to do with lavish ingredients, but has more of a spiritual stirring that occurs just before we start cooking. Yes, that's right, even before the chopping starts, a sincere intention or niyah is made for the family that graces the table, to be fed and nourished through the meal they will be served. This intention becomes a prayer, if you like, that gives thanks to a higher power for the ingredients acquired and ultimately for the sustenance they will provide. The act of cooking then becomes a form of meditation, as we continue preparing our dishes with this mantra: **Bismillah-ir-Rahman-ir-Rahim** (In the Name of God, Most Merciful, Most Compassionate).

No Cape Malay cook worth his or her salt will start cooking without this intention or continue cooking without repeating these words throughout the process. We believe with all our hearts that no matter how meagre the ingredients may seem, with the blessing from God we'll end up with more than enough to feed our families. The concept of sharing becomes essential when sitting down to eat, because food that is shared has more meaning than a simple meal eaten by one person.

Our energy flow and why the same recipe can yield different results from different cooks

To end off this chapter, I leave you with this: as human beings we are all uniquely different. Our energy flow differs from one person to another, and this also largely has to do with what we are feeling emotionally and physically. The concept of cooking with love infers that the emotions associated with love will permeate through the dish, as the energy flow of the cook is transmitted to the ingredients. This is where I become truly philosophical because, for me, this energy flow doesn't only start with me as the cook. The energy flow starts with the farmer and the labourer who planted the seeds of the herbs and ingredients I am using. I would like to believe that even at that stage a little prayer is said to yield a successful crop, and for the delicate leaves of fresh coriander or parsley to stand up against any storm it may have to face. I'm also inclined to believe that when these seeds make contact with human hands as they are placed into the soil, once again energy is transmitted and transformed.

I do not and cannot enter into cooking frivolously. I was taught that if ingredients are respected and their origins are consciously acknowledged, a greater sense of compassion and comprehension is created. The energy I have while cooking is finally transmitted as my fingertips touch the ingredients and my entire approach to the dish becomes this expression of love and passion for the art of cooking and creating.

GET GOING

CLEAN EATING TO
KICK-START YOUR DAY

There's nothing quite like a bowl of warm porridge on a chilly morning, or light Greek yoghurt loaded with chopped walnuts and a drizzle of honey, on those warmer days, to get me going in the morning. On the days when I'm pressed for time, a quick smoothie does the trick!

My inspiration for this chapter comes from Zorah Booley Samaai, who wows all of us with her stunning photography and striking food styling in her blog called Inthemidnightkitchen. She studied at Le Cordon Bleu in London and is a qualified pastry chef, ardent food photographer, content creator, food blogger and all-round foodie. Zorah shares her passion for clean eating and pastries in her blog and her book, *The Everyday Low-FODMAP Cookbook*. It's hard not to be lured into her culinary cosmos of chia puddings, gluten-free brownies and boba teas!

The recipes in this chapter are a repertoire of smoothies and healthy breakfast options that I usually enjoy most mornings, but particularly savour during Ramadan when Muslims around the world are fasting. They provide instant nourishment, and the fact that my body responds so positively to cleaner foods makes these recipes perfect for when I need a detox from fried and baked goodies.

Coconut and Dark Chocolate Chia Puddings

Chia seed puddings are super easy to make – you simply combine the chia seeds, water and a natural sweetener such as date paste, bananas or maple syrup. Add raw or toasted coconut flakes, nuts, dried fruits, or seeds and within minutes you have a nutritious quick-fix breakfast. Since the meal prep for this little chia gem is the day before, you can literally just grab (from the fridge) and go!

SERVES 2 | **PREPARATION TIME** 10 minutes | **SETTING TIME** 10 minutes or overnight

FOR THE COCONUT CHIA PUDDING (Bowl 1)

¼ C (60 ml) chia seeds
1 C (250 ml) coconut milk
½ C (125 ml) desiccated coconut
1 Tbsp (15 ml) date paste

FOR THE DARK CHOCOLATE CHIA PUDDING (Bowl 2)

¼ C (60 ml) chia seeds
1 C (250 ml) coconut milk
½ C (125 ml) desiccated coconut
1 Tbsp (15 ml) date paste or honey
¼ C (60 ml) raw cocoa powder
1 Tbsp (15 ml) almond butter
1 tsp (5 ml) ground cinnamon

FOR SERVING

2 Tbsp (30 ml) coconut yoghurt
2 tsp (10 ml) almond butter
1 tsp (5 ml) cacao nibs
¼ C (60 ml) fresh mixed berries
2–4 edible flowers, depending on size

1 Place the ingredients for both puddings in two separate bowls.
2 Mix each bowl's ingredients together and allow to stand for 10 minutes, or leave overnight in the refrigerator (see tip below).
3 When ready to serve, spoon alternating layers of each pudding into serving glasses or bowls (or enjoy separately).
4 Top with coconut yoghurt, almond butter and cacao nibs, or use different kinds of fruits, berries or even edible flowers.

CARIEMA'S TIPS

Make your own date paste: Soak 1 C (250 ml) pitted Medjool dates in ¼ C (60 ml) warm water. Allow to stand for about 30 minutes. Once the dates have softened, mash or pulse them until they form a smooth paste. The paste can be stored in the refrigerator for up to two weeks in an airtight container.

If you're planning to leave the pudding in the refrigerator overnight, add another 1 C (250 ml) coconut milk to each pudding.

Fresh Fruit Salad
with Mango Yoghurt

I love making fruit salads because all the effort (which is minimal) is in the prepping of the fruit. This fruit salad can be paired with any plain or flavoured yoghurt, and it literally takes only 15 minutes to put it all together!

SERVES 4 | **PREPARATION TIME** 15 minutes | **SETTING TIME** none

FOR THE MANGO YOGHURT

2 C (500 ml) plain yoghurt

¼ C (60 ml) ripe mango, peeled, pitted and puréed

2 Tbsp (30 ml) honey, or to taste

½ tsp (2.5 ml) vanilla extract

FOR THE FRUIT SALAD

2 C (500 ml) mango-flavoured yoghurt

2 Tbsp (30 ml) honey

½ tsp (2.5 ml) vanilla extract

1 large apple, cored and cubed (no need to peel)

1 C (250 ml) fresh blueberries

1 C (250 ml) fresh raspberries

2 C (500 ml) fresh strawberries, hulled and halved

1 C (250 ml) green or red grapes, halved

PREPARING THE YOGHURT

1 Whisk all the ingredients together and set aside in the refrigerator until needed.

PREPARING THE FRUIT SALAD

1 Combine all the fruit in a serving bowl.

2 Serve spoonfuls of fruit in individual bowls and dollop with a spoonful (or two) of the yoghurt mixture.

My Three Go-to Smoothies

Berry Banana Smoothie

A quick mix of frozen berries, banana and plain yoghurt is the perfect quick-fix, liquid meal to give me a natural energy boost in the morning!

SERVES 2 | **PREPARATION TIME** 10 minutes | **SETTING TIME** none

2 C (500 ml) frozen mixed berries
1 medium-size banana
¾ C (200 ml) Greek yoghurt
1 C (250 ml) almond milk
1 Tbsp (15 ml) honey, or to taste

1. Place all the ingredients into a blender and blend until smooth.
2. Pour the smoothie into glasses and serve.

Date and Nut Smoothie

This smoothie is a hearty breakfast in one glass. It is abundantly nutritious and provides your daily dose of fibre from the banana, dates and oats. I've also used walnuts and almonds in this recipe as they are good sources of fibre and protein.

SERVES 2 | **PREPARATION TIME** 10 minutes | **SETTING TIME** none

3 Medjool dates, pitted
6 whole walnuts
6 whole raw almonds
1 frozen banana, sliced
½ C (125 ml) rolled oats
1 tsp (5 ml) vanilla extract
2 C (500 ml) almond milk, chilled

FOR GARNISHING
1 Tbsp (15 ml) roasted flaked almonds
¼ tsp (1.25 ml) ground cinnamon

1. Place all the smoothie ingredients into a blender and blend until smooth.
2. Divide between two large glasses.
3. Garnish with flaked almonds and a sprinkle of ground cinnamon.

Evergreen Smoothie (aka Hulk Smoothie)

In the past, the only green smoothies that appealed to me were avocado smoothies. To the point where I could not go a day without one. A few kilos heavier and a chat with a personal trainer later, I soon realised that I was literally 'drinking' more calories, because avocado smoothies are known to be higher on the calorie-count side. I then substituted it for this Hulk smoothie. It still allows me to have some avocado, but with a much lower calorie count.

SERVES 2 **|** **PREPARATION TIME** 10 minutes **|** **SETTING TIME** none

1 C (250 ml) kale, stems removed
   and roughly chopped
2 C (500 ml) baby spinach leaves
½ avocado
1 banana
1 green apple, cored and cubed
   (no need to peel)
1 C (250 ml) freshly squeezed
   orange juice
1 C (250 ml) plain yoghurt
1 Tbsp (15 ml) honey, or to taste
1 C (250 ml) ice cubes
1 Tbsp (15 ml) chia seeds

1   Place all the ingredients into a blender and
    blend until smooth.
2   Pour the smoothie into glasses or cups
    and serve.

Berry Banana
Smoothie
(page 32)

Date and Nut
Smoothie
(page 32)

Evergreen Smoothie
(page 33)

Blueberry and Banana Acai Bowl

Acai (pronounced aa-saa-ee) is a small, round, deep purple-coloured berry. It looks very similar to a blackcurrant and is loaded with antioxidants. It acts as an immune booster and because of its amazing nutritional profile it is regarded as a superfruit. If you're using frozen acai, defrost for 3–5 minutes, then cut the frozen acai packet into quarters. The smaller portions make it much easier to blend. A word of caution though, don't add too much liquid to the blender. A thicker consistency is needed to create a perfect acai bowl, as opposed to an acai smoothie.

SERVES 4 | **PREPARATION TIME** 15 minutes | **SETTING TIME** none

FOR THE ACAI BOWL BASE

100 g frozen acai berries or 2 tsp (10 ml)
   acai berry powder
1 C (250 ml) frozen blueberries
1 large frozen banana, sliced
1 Tbsp (15 ml) almond butter
3 Tbsp (45 ml) almond or coconut milk

OPTIONS FOR TOPPINGS

Sliced fruit, for added texture and
   nutrients: banana, apple, berries,
   kiwi and/or granadilla.
If you prefer a crunch-factor: muesli or
   granola (I love ones loaded with nuts),
   coconut flakes, cacao nibs or a handful
   of chopped almonds or raw cashews.
Velvety and creamy texture in the form of
   satiating fats: coconut yoghurt, roughly
   chopped raw chocolate, a generous
   drizzle of peanut butter.

1 Place all the base ingredients into a blender.
2 Pulse until smooth. Don't over blend as you want to avoid a watery mixture – it must be thick enough to eat with a spoon.
3 Pour the mixture into a bowl and add the toppings of your choice.

Low-sugar Acai Bowl

I don't have much of a sweet tooth and it's one of the reasons I love this low-sugar acai bowl. It's perfect for when you want to control your sugar intake and is so refreshing in summer with a topping of sliced or shaped fruit (just don't overdo it as the fruit will increase the sugar).

SERVES 4 | **PREPARATION TIME** 15 minutes | **SETTING TIME** none

FOR THE ACAI BOWL BASE

1 frozen banana, sliced

½ C (125 ml) frozen strawberries
   or raspberries

1 Tbsp (15 ml) acai berry powder

3 Tbsp (45 ml) almond or coconut milk

1 Tbsp (15 ml) protein powder of
   your choice

1 tsp (5 ml) cacao nibs or cocoa
   powder (optional)

1 Tbsp (15 ml) natural peanut or
   almond butter (optional)

1 Tbsp (15 ml) chia seeds

OPTIONS FOR TOPPINGS

Top with fresh summer fruit, slices of
   seedless watermelon or sweet melon,
   or Asian fruit such as dragon fruit
   or star fruit

1. Place all the base ingredients into a blender.
2. Pulse until smooth. Don't over blend as you want to avoid a watery mixture – it must be thick enough to eat with a spoon.
3. Pour the mixture into a bowl and add the toppings of your choice.

CARIEMA'S TIP

Chia seeds can be used to thicken the texture of smoothies, puddings and acai bowls. Use less or more depending on the consistency you require.

Cooked Oats
with Dried Turkish Figs

I grew up eating porridge for breakfast and have such fond memories of my mom preparing oats or maize meal for us. Her version would contain butter, a good pinch of cinnamon and a drizzle of golden syrup. It was a sure way to get my brothers and me to eat our porridge! These days, I leave out the butter and golden syrup and instead add dried Turkish figs and a drizzle of honey for sweetness. You can forego the cacao nibs and substitute dark chocolate shavings.

SERVES 4 | **PREPARATION TIME** 10 minutes | **COOKING TIME** 15 minutes

2 C (500 ml) rolled oats or
    quick-cooking oats

Salt to taste

1½ C (375 ml) water

2 Tbsp (30 ml) cacao nibs

6 dried Turkish figs (4 finely chopped,
    2 thinly sliced)

⅓ C (80 ml) almond milk, or more to get
    desired consistency

Honey to taste

1. Combine the oats, salt and water in a medium-size saucepan over medium to low heat and bring to a simmer.
2. Stir in the cacao nibs and chopped figs and continue to cook for about 3 minutes, stirring occasionally, until the oats are warmed through.
3. Add the almond milk and cook for a further 2 minutes.
4. Remove from the heat and spoon into bowls. Top with the sliced figs and a drizzle of honey, and serve piping hot.

Crunchies, South African Breakfast Health Bars

The traditional South African crunchie is an oat bar combined with goodies like almond slivers, desiccated coconut and golden syrup. Very dear friends of mine, Trevor Fleurs and Amanda Fortuin, got their daughter Lisa to make these for me on one of my trips to Cape Town. Lisa then shared her recipe with me, advising that the crunchies could be made ahead and stored in an airtight container. This soon became my grab-and-go breakfast!

   This is my version of Lisa's recipe, which also contains dried, ground naartjie peel to elevate the taste even more.

SERVES 6 | **PREPARATION TIME** 15 minutes | **BAKING TIME** 50 minutes, including cooling

100 g unsalted butter (or a bit more
   if the texture is too crumbly)
2 Tbsp (30 ml) golden syrup
½ C (125 ml) white or brown sugar
¼ C (60 ml) brown sugar
½ tsp (2.5 ml) salt
2 Tbsp (30 ml) boiling water
1 tsp (5 ml) bicarbonate of soda
1 C (250 ml) desiccated coconut
¼ C (60 ml) raw almonds,
   roughly chopped
¼ C (60 ml) chopped hazelnuts,
   walnuts or pecan nuts
1 C (250 ml) rolled oats
1 C (250 ml) self-raising wheat flour
½ tsp (2.5 ml) ground cinnamon
1 Tbsp (15 ml) dried naartjie peel,
   ground to a powder (optional)

1   Preheat the oven to 180 °C.
2   Line a 20 cm × 20 cm (for thicker bars) or 30 cm × 20 cm (for thinner bars) baking tray with baking paper and set aside.
3   In a saucepan on medium heat, melt the butter, syrup, sugars and salt, until all the sugar granules have dissolved.
4   Remove the mixture from the stove, add the boiling water and bicarbonate of soda, mix well and set aside.
5   Combine all the remaining dry ingredients in a large bowl and give this a good mix.
6   Add the wet ingredients to the dry ingredients.
7   Combine to form a pliable and crumbly texture.
8   Transfer the mixture onto the prepared baking tray and press down to smooth it out and form a level base.
9   Bake at 180 °C for 10–15 minutes, then adjust the oven temperature to 140 °C and bake for another 10 minutes or until golden.
10 Allow to cool completely before cutting into squares. Serve or store in an airtight container for up to a week.

MORNING LIGHT

COMFORTING CAPE MALAY
BREAKFAST MEALS AND SWEET
INDULGENCES TO GREET THE
MORNING LIGHT

In the Middle East, the Arabic greeting in the morning is 'Sabah Al Khair', which loosely translated means 'good morning'. However, the deeper sense of this expression means 'morning light'. This sets the tone for my day, the notion that morning light has come and, with it, the promise of a new day. In a Cape Malay home, a new day starts with early morning prayers (just before dawn) and later, once the morning light has finally come, it means breakfast, and a hearty one at that! It's the reverse at night, where our day ends with food, followed by our evening prayers. Therefore, for most Cape Malays, prayer and food are intertwined – the one provides nourishment to our souls and the other to our bodies.

I didn't have to look far for inspiration for this chapter. Ammaarah Petersen, chef, entrepreneur, food blogger, restaurateur and my 'home girl', is a sure-fire choice. She owns a café in Cape Town's V&A Waterfront called Cape Malay House, where she turns Cape Malay traditional cuisine into picture-perfect masterpieces. She exudes the Cape Town Cape Malay character with her vibey and upbeat approach to life, her no-nonsense, kick-ass attitude and her zest for travel, friends, family and food. It was difficult to single out one of her recipes, because there are so many that make me drool. However, her spicy baked beans (page 54) are perfect for my version of an English breakfast and are also ideal as an accompaniment to that good-old South African braai!

Eggs Benedict
on Mashed Avocado Toast

Hollandaise sauce is one of the first sauces I was taught to make at culinary school. In fact, during the same class, we were taught how to prepare eggs for breakfast. It was also in this class where I must have poached more than a dozen eggs! To this day, I adore making (and eating) poached eggs, either on avocado toast or on an English muffin with a spicy Hollandaise sauce.

SERVES 4 | **PREPARATION TIME** 15 minutes | **COOKING TIME** 20 minutes

FOR THE MASHED AVOCADO

1 large, ripe avocado

1 tsp (5 ml) lemon juice

½ tsp (2.5 ml) salt

½ tsp (2.5 ml) freshly ground black pepper
    or dried chilli flakes

4 slices seeded bread, English muffins or
    white toast

Microgreens, for garnishing

FOR THE SPICY HOLLANDAISE SAUCE

2 egg yolks

¼ tsp (1.25 ml) salt

1 Tbsp (15 ml) lemon juice or the
    juice of ½ lemon

1 tsp (5 ml) paprika

½ tsp (2.5 ml) cayenne pepper or peri-peri

¼ C (60 ml) warm melted butter

FOR THE POACHED EGGS

3 C (750 ml) water

1 Tbsp (15 ml) white vinegar

4 eggs

PREPARING THE AVOCADO

1 Scoop the avocado flesh into a bowl and mash with
    a fork.
2 Add the lemon juice, salt and pepper. Set aside.

PREPARING THE SAUCE

1 The easiest way to make this sauce is to place the egg
    yolks, salt, lemon juice and spices into a bowl and use
    a stick blender to blend for 30 seconds.
2 Very slowly pour the melted butter into the bowl while
    blending, until the sauce transforms into a lush and
    velvety consistency. Set aside and keep warm (or reheat
    for 30 seconds just before serving).

PREPARING THE POACHED EGGS

1 Line a plate with paper towel.
2 Bring the water to a boil in a medium-size saucepan
    on high heat.
3 Add the white vinegar and reduce the heat to
    medium low.
4 Crack an egg into a small bowl and set aside.
5 Use a spoon to create a whirlpool in the saucepan of water,
    moving the water in a circular motion.
6 Slowly submerge the egg into the water and allow it
    to move with the whirlpool.

7   Do the same with the rest of the eggs.
8   Continue creating a whirlpool in the water but at a very gentle pace.
9   After about 4 minutes, remove the eggs from the water using
     a slotted spoon and set aside on the paper towel-lined plate.

ASSEMBLING THE EGGS BENEDICT

1   Place a slice of the seeded bread (or an English muffin or piece
     of toast) on a plate and spread a spoonful of the mashed
     avocado onto the bread.
2   Place an egg on top of the avocado and drizzle with
     Hollandaise sauce. Garnish with microgreens.

Fragrant French Toast
Baked in an Egg Custard

This recipe is a hybrid that brings an old-fashioned Cape Malay bread pudding together with brioche French Toast. It's prepared in the oven and should be eaten warm, as the drizzle of caramel sauce permeates through the spongy French toast pudding. It's a breakfast dish in our home and will certainly satisfy your sweet tooth in the early morn.

SERVES 4 | **PREPARATION TIME** 10 minutes | **COOKING TIME** 20 minutes

4 eggs
Pinch of salt
1 Tbsp (15 ml) castor sugar
1 C (250 ml) full-cream milk
1 tsp (5 ml) vanilla extract or essence
½ tsp (2.5 ml) ground cinnamon

¼ tsp (1.25 ml) ground cardamom (optional)
2 slices stale or day-old white bread, crusts removed and broken into tiny pieces
6–8 slices brioche, with crusts, cut into cubes
Honey, golden syrup or store-bought caramel sauce, for drizzling

1 Preheat the oven to 180 °C.
2 Grease individual glass or cast-iron ramekins with butter or nonstick spray. Set aside.
3 Place the eggs, salt, castor sugar, milk, vanilla extract, ground cinnamon, cardamom (if using) and broken pieces of bread into a mixing bowl. Use a whisk to mix all of this together to form the egg custard.
4 Divide the egg custard among the greased ramekins.
5 Dot with the cubes of brioche, dipping them into the egg custard and allowing them to peek out.
6 Place in the oven and bake for about 20 minutes or until the egg custard has set and the tops of the brioche cubes are golden.
7 Serve hot with a drizzle of honey, golden syrup, or caramel sauce.

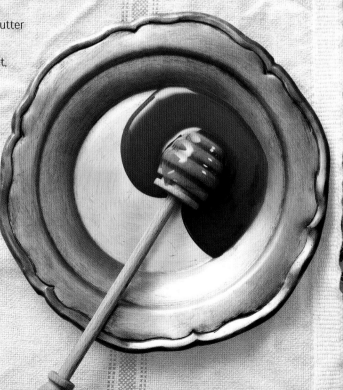

Feta, Spinach and Macon Quiche

The Halaal version of bacon is called macon in Cape Town, which is a breakfast beef strip. The macon can be replaced with chicken strips, flakes of smoked trout or salmon, or even with a medley of vegetables such as roasted brinjal, butternut or sweet potato. A serving of this quiche with a leafy green salad, and a dash of your favourite salad dressing, is a perfect start to the day.

SERVES 6 | **PREPARATION TIME** 30 minutes | **BAKING TIME** 40 minutes

FOR THE PASTRY

1 ⅓ C (330 ml) cake wheat flour , sifted
100 g salted butter, chilled
   and cut into cubes
½ Tbsp (7.5 ml) fresh thyme leaves
2 large or 3 medium egg yolks, beaten
¼ C (60 ml) chilled water

CARIEMA'S TIP

If the pastry is not completely cooked through after blind baking, remove the beans and return the tart shell to the oven for a further 5 minutes or until golden.

PREPARING THE PASTRY

1   Place the flour into the bowl of an electric mixer fitted with the hook attachment.
2   Add the cubes of butter and mix until it forms a crumbly texture.
3   Stir in the thyme leaves.
4   In a separate bowl, whisk the beaten egg yolks with the chilled water.
5   Gradually add the egg mixture to the mixing bowl and mix on a slow speed.
6   Once the dough is formed, shape it into a ball, wrap it in plastic wrap and place in the refrigerator for 20 minutes.
7   Preheat the oven to 200 °C. Spray a 25 cm-diameter pie dish with nonstick spray.
8   Remove the pastry from the fridge and roll it out on a lightly floured surface to about 3 mm thick.
9   Line the prepared pie dish with the pastry and trim off the edges.
10 Line the pastry with baking paper and fill with baking beans, then blind bake for 15–20 minutes on the middle shelf of the oven, until the pastry is slightly golden.
11 Remove the pie dish from the oven, remove the baking paper and beans and set the pastry aside to cool.

(Continued overleaf)

FOR THE FILLING

2 Tbsp (30 ml) olive oil

8–10 slices macon or breakfast beef strips, roughly chopped

1 onion, thinly sliced

1 clove garlic, peeled and crushed

400 g baby spinach leaves

3 eggs

300 ml double cream or cooking cream

140 g feta cheese, crumbled

¼ tsp (1.25 ml) salt

¼ tsp (1.25 ml) freshly ground black pepper

¼ tsp (1.25 ml) freshly grated nutmeg

PREPARING THE FILLING

1 Heat the oil in a large pan on medium to high heat.

2 Flash-fry the macon for about 3 minutes, stirring continuously. Remove from the heat and set aside on a plate.

3 Adjust the heat to medium.

4 In the same pan (no need to clean), add the sliced onion and sauté for about 10 minutes, stirring occasionally, until golden and tender.

5 Add the garlic and sauté for 2 minutes. Transfer the mixture to a bowl.

6 Again using the same pan, sauté the baby spinach on medium heat until it is wilted. Once wilted, leave it to cool then squeeze out the excess liquid.

7 In a large mixing bowl, whisk the eggs and cream together until velvety.

8 Stir in three-quarters of the feta cheese, as well as the salt, pepper and nutmeg.

ASSEMBLING THE QUICHE

1 Preheat the oven to 180 ºC.

2 Spread the onion mixture on the base of the pastry shell and crumble over the remaining feta.

3 Spread the baby spinach over the feta and onions, then scatter over the macon. Carefully pour over the egg and cream mixture.

4 Bake on the middle shelf of the oven for 20 minutes. To check if the filling is cooked through, give the dish a little shake – if the filling is still wobbly, give it another 5 minutes.

5 Remove from the oven, leave to cool slightly and serve warm or at room temperature.

Cape Malay English Breakfast Bowl

An English breakfast in a Cape Malay household must have a spicy element in one or two of the ingredients. Most often it is a spicy breakfast sausage or spicy baked beans. My version is inspired by the Cape Malay chef Ammaarah Petersen. It's loaded with just enough heat to wake up your tastebuds in the morning and the fresh garlic and green chillies elevate the taste of the store-bought baked beans. This dish also makes for a piquant side to our much-loved braais. I also do a variation that includes portions of sausage and I serve it on a slice of toast – it's quick comfort food with minimal effort!

SERVES 4 | **PREPARATION TIME** 10 minutes | **COOKING TIME** 20 minutes

FOR THE MUSHROOMS
1 Tbsp (15 ml) canola or vegetable oil
1 punnet (250 g) mixed mushrooms, sliced
½ tsp (2.5 ml) salt
½ tsp (2.5 ml) freshly ground black pepper

FOR THE SPICY BAKED BEANS
1 Tbsp (15 ml) canola or vegetable oil
2 fresh curry leaves (optional)
1 onion, finely sliced
1 clove garlic, peeled and crushed
½ tsp (2.5 ml) salt
1 tsp (5 ml) ground cumin
1 tsp (5 ml) roasted masala or curry powder
½ tsp (2.5 ml) kokni masala or chilli powder
2 cans (410 g each) baked beans in tomato sauce
1–2 fresh green chillies, thinly sliced

FOR SERVING
2 C (500 ml) baby spinach leaves, cooked until wilted
4 fried eggs
8 breakfast sausages, fried or grilled
4 sprigs fresh coriander

PREPARING THE MUSHROOMS
1 Heat the oil in a saucepan on medium to high heat.
2 Add the mushrooms and adjust the heat to high.
3 Sauté for 5–7 minutes or until the mushrooms are slightly golden. Season, then set aside and keep warm.

PREPARING THE SPICY BAKED BEANS
1 Heat the oil in a saucepan on medium to high heat.
2 Add the curry leaves (if using) and fry for about 30 seconds, then add the onion, garlic and salt.
3 Sauté for 5–7 minutes or until the onion is slightly golden.
4 Add all the spices and sauté for a minute, just until the spices release their natural oils and aromas.
5 Adjust the heat to low and add the canned baked beans and slices of green chilli.
6 Simmer on low heat for 3–5 minutes.

ASSEMBLING THE BOWL

1. Layer each bowl with baby spinach leaves, then a scoop of mushrooms.
2. Drizzle one spoon of beans over the mushrooms, then add the fried egg and sausages.
3. Drizzle over a last few spoons of spicy beans and serve.

Feriel Sonday's Heavenly Cape Malay Bollas

Feriel Sonday has a very successful Facebook page entitled Feriel Sonday's Heavenly Bites where she shares her much-loved recipes with her devoted followers. Her recipe makes *the* perfect Cape Malay bollas, and by perfect I mean the lightest, fluffiest vanilla-infused bollas! The recipe calls for four cups of flour and I was tempted to make half the batter, thinking it would be way too much for my family to consume in one go. I was grossly mistaken – these heavenly bites had them coming back for seconds and thirds!

FOR THE SUGAR SYRUP

2 C (500 ml) water
2½ C (625 ml) white sugar

FOR THE BATTER

4 C (4 × 250 ml) cake wheat flour
4 tsp (20 ml) baking powder
2 eggs
¾ C (200 ml) white sugar
1 tsp (5 ml) vanilla or caramel essence
¾ C (200 ml) canola or vegetable oil
Pinch of salt
2 C (500 ml) buttermilk

FOR FINISHING

3 C (750 ml) canola or vegetable oil for
   deep-frying, or more depending on the
   size of the saucepan
1 C (250 ml) desiccated coconut

PREPARING THE SUGAR SYRUP

1   Bring the water to a boil in a medium-size saucepan on
   high heat.
2   Add the sugar and boil for 7–10 minutes or until the
   sugar has completely dissolved and the sugar syrup has
   thickened slightly. Set aside.

PREPARING THE BATTER

1   In a bowl, sift the flour and baking powder twice and then
   set aside.
2   Place the eggs and sugar into the bowl of an electric mixer
   fitted with the paddle attachment, and mix until light
   and fluffy.
3   Add the vanilla essence and oil, and mix until creamy.
4   Gradually add half of the sifted flour, the salt and half
   of the buttermilk, and mix.
5   Add the rest of the flour and buttermilk and continue
   mixing to form a smooth batter.
6   Set aside for at least 30 minutes before frying.

PREPARING THE BOLLAS

1   Line a plate with paper towel and set aside.
2   Heat the oil for deep-frying in a medium-size saucepan
   on medium to high heat for 12–15 minutes. (Drop a small
   teaspoon of the batter into the hot oil – if it floats to the
   top, the oil is ready.)
3   Place tablespoonsful of the batter into the hot oil
   and fry until golden brown, turning halfway.
4   Remove the bollas from the oil with a slotted spoon
   and set aside on the paper towel-lined plate.
5   Reheat the syrup on a medium heat and drop about four
   bollas into the hot syrup.
6   Coat with the syrup until glossy, then set aside on a
   serving plate or platter and sprinkle with the
   desiccated coconut.

Mom's Breakfast Flapjacks

This was one of my mom's signature recipes and if we didn't have these for breakfast, they would make their appearance on a Sunday for afternoon tea. These little gems are airy and light, simply served with sweet, crimson strawberry jam and a dollop of clotted cream.

SERVES 6 | **PREPARATION TIME** 15 minutes | **COOKING TIME** 40 minutes, including resting time

FOR THE BATTER

2 C (500 ml) cake wheat flour
1 tsp (5 ml) bicarbonate of soda
2 tsp (10 ml) baking powder
3 Tbsp (45 ml) castor or white sugar
Pinch of salt
2 eggs, beaten
1¼ C (310 ml) buttermilk
½ C (125 ml) sour cream
50 g unsalted butter, melted and cooled
1 tsp (5 ml) vanilla essence

FOR SERVING

Strawberry jam and clotted cream, double
    cream or whipped cream

PREPARING THE BATTER

1 Sift the flour, bicarbonate of soda, baking powder, sugar and salt together in a large mixing bowl. Set aside.
2 Place the eggs, buttermilk, sour cream, melted butter and vanilla essence into a separate bowl and whisk until smooth.
3 Add the wet ingredients to the dry ingredients and gently fold together. Be careful not to over mix to ensure a light and airy batter.
4 Allow the batter to rest for about 10 minutes.

PREPARING THE FLAPJACKS

1 Place a nonstick pan on medium heat. If you don't have a nonstick pan, then spray the pan with nonstick spray or drizzle with a teaspoon of oil before frying.
2 Drop tablespoonsful of the batter into the pan and cook until bubbles begin to form on the surface.
3 Flip the flapjack over and cook until lightly browned on the bottom.
4 Serve warm with strawberry jam and cream.

CARIEMA'S TIP

Chocolate Chip Flapjacks: Drop a spoonful of the batter into the pan, sprinkle with white or milk chocolate chips. Turn the flapjacks over when ready and cook until finished.

SANDWICH SENSATION

NO 'SUB'-STITUTE
FOR A SENSATIONAL SARMIE

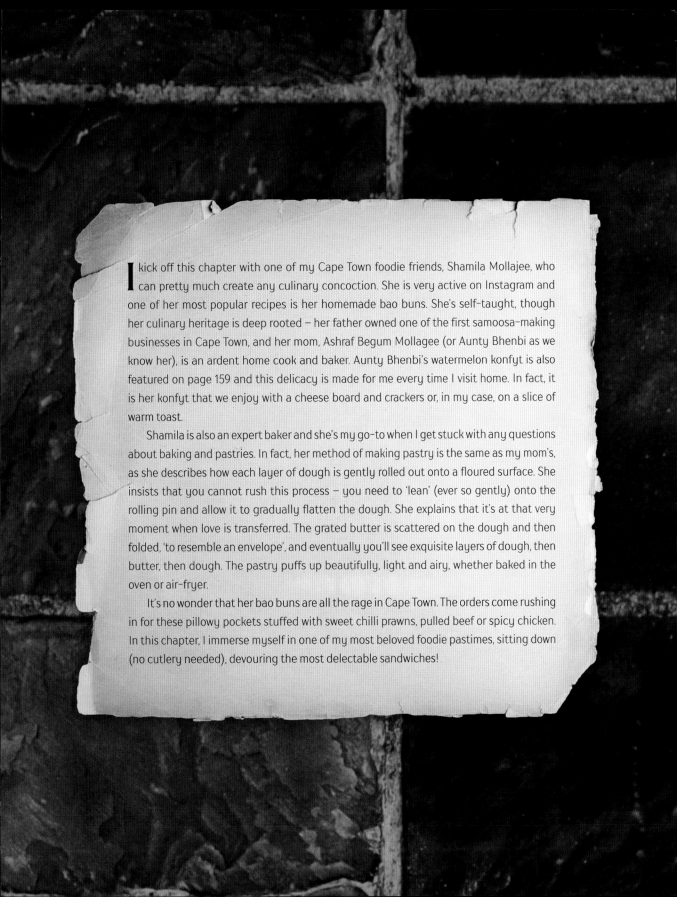

I kick off this chapter with one of my Cape Town foodie friends, Shamila Mollajee, who can pretty much create any culinary concoction. She is very active on Instagram and one of her most popular recipes is her homemade bao buns. She's self-taught, though her culinary heritage is deep rooted – her father owned one of the first samoosa-making businesses in Cape Town, and her mom, Ashraf Begum Mollagee (or Aunty Bhenbi as we know her), is an ardent home cook and baker. Aunty Bhenbi's watermelon konfyt is also featured on page 159 and this delicacy is made for me every time I visit home. In fact, it is her konfyt that we enjoy with a cheese board and crackers or, in my case, on a slice of warm toast.

Shamila is also an expert baker and she's my go-to when I get stuck with any questions about baking and pastries. In fact, her method of making pastry is the same as my mom's, as she describes how each layer of dough is gently rolled out onto a floured surface. She insists that you cannot rush this process – you need to 'lean' (ever so gently) onto the rolling pin and allow it to gradually flatten the dough. She explains that it's at that very moment when love is transferred. The grated butter is scattered on the dough and then folded, 'to resemble an envelope', and eventually you'll see exquisite layers of dough, then butter, then dough. The pastry puffs up beautifully, light and airy, whether baked in the oven or air-fryer.

It's no wonder that her bao buns are all the rage in Cape Town. The orders come rushing in for these pillowy pockets stuffed with sweet chilli prawns, pulled beef or spicy chicken. In this chapter, I immerse myself in one of my most beloved foodie pastimes, sitting down (no cutlery needed), devouring the most delectable sandwiches!

Shamila Mollajee's Bao Buns

Shamila's baos are modelled after the traditional Asian bao bun – made from flour dough, cut out in circular shapes, and then folded over, steamed and filled with meat and other ingredients. The buns are pillowy soft, which she credits to the tangzhong, an Asian technique where a small percentage of the flour and liquid is added to a yeast recipe or dish.

MAKES 14–16 | **PREPARATION TIME** 30 minutes | **COOKING TIME** 2 hours 30 minutes, including resting time

FOR THE BUNS

1 C (250 ml) warm water
½ tsp (2.5 ml) instant dry yeast
1 Tbsp (15 ml) white sugar
2 Tbsp (30 ml) canola or vegetable oil
2⅓ C (580 ml) cake wheat flour
2 Tbsp (30 ml) powdered milk or
   coffee creamer
1 tsp (5 ml) baking powder
Pinch of salt

FOR THE TANGZHONG

1⅓ C (330 ml) warm water
2 Tbsp (30 ml) cake wheat flour

FOR THE PRAWN FILLING

1 Tbsp (15 ml) olive or canola oil
42–48 medium prawns, shelled, tail on or off, and deveined
2 Tbsp (30 ml) sweet chilli sauce
1 tsp (5 ml) chilli paste (optional)
1 C (250 ml) fresh bean sprouts
1 C (250 ml) finely shredded red cabbage
½ C (125 ml) Japanese mayonnaise or any mayo
   of your choosing

PREPARING THE BUNS

1 In a bowl, combine the warm water, yeast, sugar and oil and whisk until the sugar has dissolved. Set aside for 5–10 minutes or until the yeast has bloomed.
2 Place the ingredients for the tangzhong into a small bowl and whisk together until smooth. Set aside.
3 Place the flour, powdered milk or coffee creamer, baking powder and salt into the bowl of an electric mixer fitted with the hook attachment.
4 Add the wet ingredients, including the tangzhong, to the dry ingredients. Mix on a slow speed for about 1 minute.
5 Adjust the speed to medium and mix for about 2 minutes, until the dough is formed. The dough should be elastic and soft but not stick to your fingers or to the sides of the mixing bowl.
6 Remove the dough from the bowl and form it into a ball.

7   Dip a pastry brush in oil and brush the surface of the mixing bowl
    with oil. Place the dough back into the mixing bowl and cover with
    plastic wrap. Set aside to rise in a warm spot for about 1 hour until it
    has more than doubled in size.

8   Place the risen dough on a clean work surface. It's not necessary to flour
    the surface, but if you do, use as little flour as possible. Roll out the dough
    to 5 mm thick. Use a glass or round cookie cutter to cut out the baos.

9   Lightly brush or spray oil on one surface of the baos and fold in half to
    make a half-moon shape. Gently press each bao with a roller and place
    on individually cut baking paper. Cover with a kitchen towel and allow
    to rest for 30 minutes before steaming.

10 Meanwhile, bring water to a boil in a wok or pot. Carefully place the baos
    with the baking paper into the steamer and cover with the steamer's lid.

11 Steam over the boiling water for about 8 minutes, making sure the water
    doesn't touch the baos.

12 When they are done cooking, tilt the lid slightly to allow air to circulate
    for 2–3 minutes.

PREPARING THE PRAWNS

1   Heat the oil in a medium-size frying pan on medium to high heat.

2   Add the prawns and sauté for 3–5 minutes or until the flesh is opaque.
    Add the sweet chilli sauce and chilli paste (if using)
    to the pan and toss until the prawns are coated in the sauce. Set aside.

ASSEMBLING THE BUNS

1   Open the fold of the bao bun and place three prawns, bean sprouts and
    shredded cabbage attractively. Drizzle with mayonnaise and serve.

Tash's Smash Beef Burger Sliders

My youngest son, Tashreeq, introduced us to the concept of a smash burger, which is an American-inspired beef burger patty. The beef mince is shaped into balls that are placed on a hot grill, then pressed or smashed with a burger press or an egg lifter to resemble a patty. I customised these burgers into sliders, because they are great to serve at dinners or lunches with friends or family.

SERVES 6 | **PREPARATION TIME** 30 minutes | **COOKING TIME** 40 minutes

FOR THE CARAMELISED ONIONS

1 Tbsp (15 ml) olive oil

2 Tbsp (30 ml) salted butter

2 medium-size onions, sliced into rings

FOR THE SLIDERS

1.2 kg minced beef steak (either rib-eye, rump or sirloin – I've used Angus beef for this recipe)

1 tsp (5 ml) freshly ground black pepper

1 tsp (5 ml) salt

¼ C (60 ml) basting sauce of choice

6 slices Cheddar cheese, cut into quarters

12 slider or dinner rolls

Slices of pickled jalapeño, gherkins or cucumber

Thin slices pineapple (optional)

PREPARING THE CARAMELISED ONIONS

1 Heat the oil and butter in a large pan on high heat.

2 Add the onion rings and sauté for about 3 minutes until translucent. Reduce the heat to medium and fry the onions for about 12 minutes until the edges are a dark golden colour. Set aside.

PREPARING THE SLIDERS

1 Shape the minced beef into 24 golf ball-size portions.

2 Place a cast-iron pan or griddle on the stovetop or grill, on high heat, until smoke is coming off the pan/griddle.

3 Place two to four burgers at a time on the hot surface, smashing with a metal burger press or egg lifter to form a thin patty. Sprinkle with salt and pepper and baste lightly with the basting sauce.

4 Cook for 2–3 minutes then flip, sprinkle with salt and pepper, and baste again. Add a cheese slice per patty.

5 Once the cheese has melted, remove the patties from the pan/griddle. Stack one patty on top of another, then keep warm until needed. Repeat until all sliders are done.

ASSEMBLING THE SLIDERS

1 Place the patties on the slider buns and top with caramelised onions, slices of pickled jalapeño, gherkins or cucumber, or thin slices of pineapple. Enjoy!

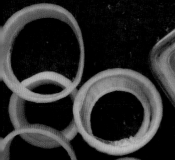

Tawfeeq's Manoushe
with Chicken and Avocado Filling

My eldest son, Tawfeeq, loves Lebanese flatbreads, a result of living in Dubai where manoushe (singular for flatbread) or manakeesh (plural) are abundantly available. Since I don't always have the time to make the bread from scratch, a store-bought wrap also works perfectly. This recipe is pretty much all the things he adores as a filling – cheese, chicken and avocado.

SERVES 4 | **PREPARATION TIME** 30 minutes | **COOKING TIME** 30 minutes

FOR THE YOGHURT SAUCE
½ C (125 ml) plain yoghurt
1 Tbsp (15 ml) mayonnaise
2 Tbsp (30 ml) tahini (optional)
½ Tbsp (7.5 ml) olive oil
Juice of ½ lemon
1 small clove garlic, crushed (optional)
Salt to taste

FOR THE FILLING
1 Tbsp (15 ml) canola or sunflower oil
2 chicken breast fillets, thinly sliced
1 clove garlic, peeled and crushed
1 tsp (5 ml) paprika
½ tsp (2.5 ml) freshly ground black pepper
Salt to taste
1 tsp (5 ml) harissa or chilli paste
½ Tbsp (7.5 ml) tomato paste
1 tsp (5 ml) white sugar
¼ C (60 ml) water

FOR FINISHING
4 large wraps
1 C (250 ml) grated mozzarella cheese
2 ripe avocados, peeled, pitted and sliced
Fresh parsley, mint, or both, for garnishing

PREPARING THE SAUCE
1 Combine all the sauce ingredients in a bowl, then set aside in the refrigerator.

PREPARING THE FILLING
1 Heat the oil in a large pan on medium to high heat.
2 Add the sliced chicken and garlic and sauté for 5–7 minutes or until the chicken is slightly golden.
3 Add the paprika, pepper, salt, harissa or chilli paste, tomato paste, sugar and water, and give this a good mix.
4 Cook for about 5 minutes more, then switch off the stove but leave the chicken on the warm stovetop.

ASSEMBLING THE WRAPS
1 Scatter the grated mozzarella cheese in the centre of each wrap, then add avocado slices followed by the warm chicken. Bring the side edges of the wrap together and fold over the top and bottom edges to resemble a parcel.
2 Place the folded wraps in a panini press or hot nonstick pan and toast until lightly golden and crispy on the outside.
3 Slice in half and then drizzle with the yoghurt sauce, either inside or outside the wrap. Garnish with the herbs and serve with a fresh green, leafy salad and light dressing.

My Mom's Chicken Mayo Sandwich

One of my late mom's favourite sandwiches was an old-fashioned chicken mayo made with Crosse and Blackwell mayonnaise. It wasn't until I moved to the Middle East that I realised just how much I loved this sandwich, especially since the ones I had abroad didn't have the same flavour profile. The mayo is the game changer and my preference is Crosse and Blackwell, but use your own favourite mayo.

SERVES 2 | **PREPARATION TIME** 15 minutes | **ASSEMBLY TIME** 10 minutes

FOR THE CHICKEN MAYO FILLING

2 chicken breasts, cooked and cubed
   (leftover roast chicken is perfect)
½ C (125 ml) mayonnaise
½ tsp (2.5 ml) salt, or to taste
½ tsp (2.5 ml) white or black pepper
½ tsp (2.5 ml) paprika or dried chilli flakes

FOR FINISHING

4 slices bread of your choosing
   (I've used seeded bread)
Microgreens, for garnishing (optional)
Butter, for spreading

PREPARING THE FILLING

1 Mix all the filling ingredients together in a bowl. Set aside.

ASSEMBLING THE SANDWICH

1 For an open sandwich, place dollops of chicken mayo on slices of your favourite bread. Sprinkle with additional chilli flakes or paprika and garnish with microgreens.

2 For a toasted sandwich, butter each slice of bread on one side.

3 Place a generous scoop of chicken mayo on the unbuttered side of the bread.

4 Heat a pan on high heat. Place the slice with the filling in the hot pan and reduce the heat to medium. Place the other slice on top with the buttered side facing up.

5 Gently toast the sandwich and be careful not to push down too hard otherwise the chicken mayo may come out of the sandwich. Flip the sandwich over and toast the other side.

6 Portion the sandwich and serve with sliced avocado or a fresh green salad.

Masala Steak Sandwich

Masala steak sandwiches are synonymous with Cape Town street food. This recipe incorporates flavours from all the take-away cafés where I've eaten this sandwich – Wembley Roadhouse in Belgravia Road, Athlone; Busy Corner in Wynberg; The Lounge in Kromboom, and let's not forget the legendary Mariam's Kitchen in the city centre! A standard sandwich will contain morsels of tender steak, cooked in a spicy and lush masala sauce, cocooned between two thick slices of white bread. The outside facing slices of bread are then coated with butter (not margarine) and toasted until golden and crisp!

SERVES 2 | **PREPARATION TIME** 30 minutes | **COOKING TIME** 40 minutes

FOR THE MASALA STEAK FILLING

500 g rump or sirloin steak, sliced into
   palm-size portions and tenderised
1 tsp (5 ml) meat tenderiser powder
½ Tbsp (7.5 ml) ginger and garlic paste
1 Tbsp (15 ml) vegetable or canola oil
½ tsp (2.5 ml) black mustard seeds
1 onion, very finely chopped
1 tomato, skinned and grated
1 tsp (5 ml) roasted masala or
   Pakco curry powder
1 tsp (5 ml) kokni masala
   or ½ tsp (2.5 ml) chilli powder
¼ tsp (1.25 ml) dried chilli flakes
½ tsp (2.5 ml) freshly ground black pepper
¼ tsp (1.25 ml) turmeric
1 tsp (5 ml) ground cumin
1 tsp (5 ml) tomato paste
1 tsp (5 ml) white sugar
Salt to taste (do a taste test first because
   the meat tenderiser contains salt)

FOR FINISHING

Butter, for spreading
4 slices white bread

PREPARING THE FILLING

1 Place the steak slices into a bowl and coat them with the meat tenderiser, and garlic and ginger paste. Set aside for 10 minutes.
2 Heat the oil in a medium pan on a medium to high heat.
3 When the oil is hot, add the mustard seeds and, once they start popping, add the onion and tomato. Sauté for about 2 minutes, then add all the spices and give this a good mix. Cook for about 3 minutes on medium heat.
4 Add the tomato paste and sugar and mix until the sugar has dissolved. Add the steak and coat liberally with the cooked ingredients. Cook, covered, for 25–30 minutes or until the steak is tender. Set aside.

ASSEMBLING THE SANDWICH

1 Butter each slice of bread on one side.
2 Place a generous scoop of masala steak on the unbuttered side of the bread.
3 Heat a pan on high heat. Place the slice with the filling in the hot pan and reduce the heat to medium. Place the other slice on top with the buttered side facing up.
4 Gently toast the sandwich and be careful not to push down too hard otherwise the filling may come out of the sandwich. Flip the sandwich over and toast the other side.
5 Portion the sandwich and serve with chips.

The Iconic Gatsby

One cannot gloss over this iconic Cape Town sandwich without understanding exactly what all the hype is about when it comes to the Gatsby. Heritage cuisine in South Africa is an integral part of the identity of our rainbow nation. In Cape Town, the street food culture is the heartbeat of the Mother City and the Gatsby remains the most iconic.

The name itself might have been influenced slightly by the 1925 novel, *The Great Gatsby* by American writer F. Scott Fitzgerald, for its depiction of a larger-than-life variation of the American dream. In the case of the Cape Town Gatsby, *larger than life* certainly comes to mind when you consider that this bulky sandwich can easily feed four to six people, generously!

In the heart of the southern suburbs in Cape town, Mr Rashaad Pandy, the inventor of the original Gatsby, maintains that it was accidentally created by him and was never supposed to have been on their menu at Super Fisheries in Athlone. According to Mr Pandy, *'he serendipitously invented the gatsby in the 70s after putting together a few odds and ends comprising of a Portuguese roll, hot chips, polony and atchar to feed a few hungry workers.'* He goes on to mention that it seemed to have been a hit and he decided to make a few more the following day, left it out for customers to sample and to provide feedback. The name itself was suggested by a friend and longtime customer, who confirmed that this mega sandwich was a 'smash – in fact a *Gatsby* smash!'. Mr Pandy loved it and the Gatsby as we know it was born.

The essence of a great Gatsby is the combination of fluffy bread, salty and zesty slap chips, cold meats or masala steak and spicy sauce. The bread cannot be crusty, it has to be soft and fluffy to soak up all the flavours. The chips must be the traditional slap chips that most South Africans adore, drenched in vinegar and sprinkled with salt.

The quality and quantity of the meat are essential. The most common are cold meats such as polonies or viennas, or tenderised cuts of beef such as braised steak or masala steak. In terms of quantity, you need a good balance of meat and chips to bread. This also brings me to the sauce, which provides added flavour and moisture. The sauce is down to individual taste, but is as crucial as all the other elements I have mentioned here. The more popular sauces are the spicy, red chilli- and peri-peri-based tomato sauces. These are just a few of a variety of sauces that one can choose from, including a selection of atchars. The fillings range from fish, chicken and seafood to the full house, which consists of masala steak, fried eggs and cheese! The Gatsby is also garnished with crispy iceberg lettuce and slices of ripe, red tomatoes. Lastly, before your order is finally packaged, you'll be asked *'how do you want it sliced?'*. Your answer really depends on how many people will be devouring this mega sandwich! The standard response is often 'sliced into four or six pieces' but even an ambitious eight pieces can be accommodated.

SERVES 6 | **PREPARATION TIME** 20 minutes | **COOKING TIME** 20 minutes

FOR THE SAUCE

2 Tbsp (30 ml) vinegar

¼ C (60 ml) tomato sauce

¼ C (60 ml) sweet chilli sauce

½ Tbsp (7.5 ml) seasoning salt
  (I've used the Taj's chips salt)

½ tsp (2.5 ml) peri-peri

1 tsp (5 ml) paprika

½ tsp (2.5 ml) roasted masala
  or curry powder

1 tsp (5 ml) white sugar (optional)

FOR THE SANDWICH

8 C (2 litres) canola or vegetable oil,
  for deep-frying

10 large potatoes, peeled and cut into
  chips and soaked in 3 C (750 ml) water

16 slices French or garlic polony
  or 12 red viennas

1 large soft baguette, sliced down
  the centre but still intact at the back
  of the loaf

2 ripe tomatoes, sliced

6 iceberg lettuce leaves

PREPARING THE SAUCE

1   Mix all the ingredients together in a bowl and set aside.

PREPARING THE COLD MEAT AND CHIPS

1   Prepare a large baking tray by placing sheets of paper towel on the bottom. This will assist in draining excess oil when transferring the hot chips from the oil.

2   Also line a plate with paper towel. This will assist in draining excess oil when transferring the cold meats from the hot oil.

3   Heat the oil in a large saucepan on high heat.

4   In the meantime, drain the potato chips and pat them dry with a kitchen towel.

5   Once the oil is hot, drop the raw potato chips into the oil and deep-fry for 15–20 minutes or until the chips are golden and tender.

6   Remove the fried chips with a slotted spoon and transfer to the paper towel-lined baking tray.

7   Drop the polony slices or viennas into the oil for literally just a minute and remove, then set aside on the paper towel-lined plate.

8   Once most of the excess oil has been drained, transfer the chips into a large mixing bowl.

9   Pour the sauce over the chips and toss until the chips are well coated.

ASSEMBLING THE GATSBY

1   Place the baguette on a cutting board while you assemble the sandwich.

2   Generously cover the bottom half of the bread with chips, spreading them out to cover the entire surface of the bread.

3   Liberally place the fried polony or viennas on top of the chips. You can, at this stage, also add additional sauce of your choosing.

4   Add the last layer of chips, then lettuce leaves and slices of tomato. Slice into six portions and serve.

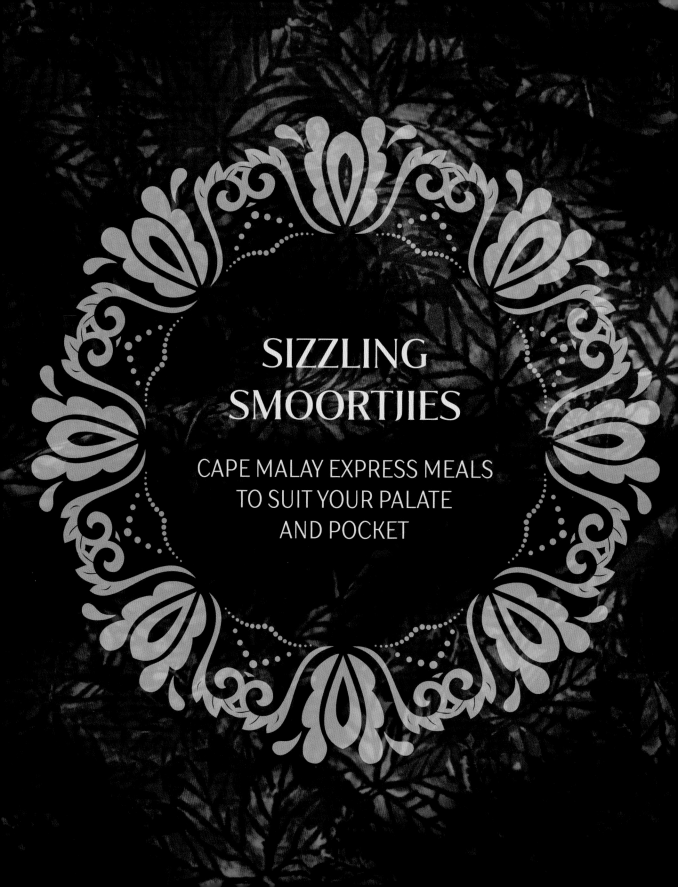

SIZZLING SMOORTJIES

CAPE MALAY EXPRESS MEALS
TO SUIT YOUR PALATE
AND POCKET

This chapter is inspired by two Cape Malay home cooks and very successful food bloggers, namely Salwaa Smith, cookbook author and food blogger of Cape Malay Cooking & Other Delights, and Fatima Sydow, from the television series and cookbooks *Kaap, Kerrie & Koesisters*. Salwaa attributes her cooking and baking skills to her late mother, Zainunesa Francis (née Adams), who was an ardent cook and, beyond their home, cooked and baked for the community and for fundraisers. Salwaa now resides in Birmingham, England, where she's wowed the locals with her Cape Malay cooking and other delights. Fatima Sydow cooks and bakes in honour of her late mother, Wasiela Sydow, who Fatima remembers fondly as always welcoming friends, family and neighbours to their home for a bite to eat. It's also evident through Fatima's recollection of home cooking that it didn't matter whether a handful or an abundance of ingredients was available, her mom turned no one away.

Both Fatima and Salwaa boast more than five hundred thousand followers on their individual Facebook pages and happily share their traditional Cape Malay recipes and stories. Their stories of home and food are intertwined with a remarkable connectedness to recollections of their families' home kitchens, religious and celebratory festivities and the recipes that have been passed down to them. It's also on both of their social media feeds and pages where the word 'smoortjies' can easily be found. You'll see a myriad recipes and images, and thousands of comments from their devoted followers who relate to eating and preparing a smoortjie.

The term 'smoor' is derived from the Indonesian word 'semur' and is also connected to the Dutch word 'smoor', which means stewing or braising. A dish like 'semur daging' is a stewed beef dish with a heavy Dutch influence. In Indonesia and Malaysia, beef is the preferred meat of choice. The Malaysians in particular love a peppery beef-steak dish that is the equivalent of the Cape Malay braised steak (gesmoore steak) and, like the Malaysians, the steak is braised with salt, pepper and onions. Nothing else needed!

I've always maintained that if bredies are the heart of Cape Malay cooking, then smoortjies are its soul! When trying to explain a smoortjie to anyone in English, we more often than not revert to the term 'braised', i.e. braised chops, braised sausage or braised egg. But a smoortjie is so much more than that and represents more than food to me. It depicts a period of time during the month when we were running low on groceries and pay day was still a few days away. I also know a smoortjie to be something that takes almost no time to make and is ideal for a quick lunch or dinner solution when unexpected guests arrive. Most smoortjies have base ingredients such as onions, tomato and garlic, with the possible addition of a green chilli. The dish itself has a lovely saucy gravy and, depending on which time of the month it was made, you could be cooking anything from Braised Steak or Braised Penny Polonies to Braised Tuna or Braised Egg. Smoortjies were also usually served with fresh white bread, thus making the perfect filling for sandwiches. However, the humble smoortjie is also ideal as a topping on crackers or a potato spud, and even as a savoury filling in pastries.

Suffice to say, this traditional dish has stood the test of time and its importance in the Cape Malay culinary recipe vault should be treasured and revered.

Cape Malay Masala Scrambled Eggs (Polla)

This is a very traditional Cape Malay egg dish that I also remember having as a filling on my school lunchtime sandwiches and on jaffels when we went on family outings to the beach or picnics. If you are having it as a sit-down meal, then be mindful not to overcook the eggs because they should be moist, not dry. It's best to serve this dish immediately, straight out of the pan!

SERVES 4 | **PREPARATION TIME** 10 minutes | **COOKING TIME** 20 minutes

2 Tbsp (30 ml) cooking oil
1 medium-size onion, thinly sliced
½ tsp (2.5 ml) salt
1 medium-size tomato, finely chopped
1 clove garlic, peeled and crushed
1–2 fresh green chillies, finely chopped
1 tsp (5 ml) white sugar
½ tsp (2.5 ml) turmeric
1 tsp (5 ml) ground cumin
1 tsp (5 ml) roasted masala or curry powder
½ tsp (2.5 ml) kokni masala or chilli powder
8 large eggs, beaten
1 fresh red chilli, thinly sliced,
    for garnishing
Baby spinach leaves, for garnishing

1. Heat the oil in a large pan on medium to high heat.
2. Add the onion and salt and sauté for 3–5 minutes or until the onion is slightly golden.
3. Reduce the heat to medium and add the chopped tomato, garlic, green chilli and sugar, and cook for 10 minutes.
4. Add all the spices and sauté for about 2 minutes or until the spices release their natural oils and aromas.
5. Add the beaten eggs and swirl all the ingredients together with a spatula or wooden spoon. Don't over mix.
6. Reduce the heat to low and place a lid on the pan. Cook gently for about 3 minutes.
7. Remove the lid, give the ingredients one last swirl, then garnish with the red chilli slices and baby spinach leaves and serve hot with Braised Sausage (page 80), bread or crusty rolls.

CARIEMA'S TIP

You can jazz up the spicy scrambled eggs even further by swirling dollops of cream cheese or goat's milk cheese into the warm, almost cooked scrambled eggs. For added decadence/indulgence, (using a cast iron pan) sprinkle generously with grated cheddar or parmesan cheese and pop under a hot grill or salamander just until the cheese starts to blister, then serve.

Braised Sausage
(Gesmore Soeseis)

Cape Town boasts some of the finest Halaal butcheries around that specialise not only in a wide variety of sausages, but also cocktail sausages and cold meats such as viennas, polonies and penny polonies. For Cape Malays, this dish is most authentic when made with sausages from local Halaal butcheries and to this day is made at least once if not twice per week! If the sausage is spicy, then omit the chilli and pepper in this recipe. Salt is optional or to taste, as some of the sausages have added salt and seasoning.

SERVES 6 | **PREPARATION TIME** 15 minutes | **COOKING TIME** 1 hour

2 Tbsp (30 ml) sunflower or canola oil

2 large onions, finely chopped

1 ripe tomato, roughly chopped

1 fresh green chilli, split lengthwise

1 tsp (5 ml) white sugar

Salt to taste

2 C (500 ml) water

½ Tbsp (7.5 ml) tomato paste

3–4 medium-size potatoes, peeled
    and quartered

1 kg sausage, cut into thumb-size portions

½ tsp (2.5 ml) freshly ground black pepper

1   Heat the oil in a large saucepan on medium-high to high heat and add the chopped onions.

2   Sauté for 5–7 minutes, stirring frequently, then add the chopped tomato, chilli and sugar. Adjust the heat to medium and sauté for 15 minutes, stirring occasionally.

3   Just as the onions and tomato are about to catch on the bottom of the saucepan, add ¼ C (60 ml) of the water and cook for a further 5 minutes.

4   Add ½ C (125 ml) of water, the tomato paste and potatoes and give this a good stir. Cook, covered, for about 10 minutes on medium heat until the liquid has transformed into a lush sauce.

5   Place the sausage portions on top of the potatoes – do not stir! Adjust the heat to high and cook, covered, for 5 minutes.

6   Add the rest of the water, adjust the heat to medium and cook, covered, for about 20 minutes.

7   Sprinkle with pepper and fold everything together. This is to ensure that the sausages and potatoes are well coated with sauce and that everything has come together. You can add a little water if you prefer a slightly thinner sauce.

8   Serve hot with fresh bread or fluffy white rice.

Braised Chicken Livers
(Gesmore Chicken Livers)

This has become a weekend treat in our home, and one that is served with anything from leftover rice to bread or crackers. If you're on a tight budget but want to glam up this smoortjie, serve it on a bed of 2-minute noodles and drizzle with sweet chilli sauce or your choice of Nando's sauces!

SERVES 4 | **PREPARATION TIME** 10 minutes | **COOKING TIME** 25 minutes

2 Tbsp (30 ml) sunflower or canola oil

1 onion, finely sliced

1 clove garlic, peeled and crushed

500 g chicken livers, cleaned and halved

½ tsp (2.5 ml) freshly ground black pepper

1 tsp (5 ml) ground cumin

1 tsp (5 ml) roasted masala or
  curry powder

½ tsp (2.5 ml) lemon juice

1 tsp (5 ml) tomato paste

1 tsp (5 ml) white sugar

Salt to taste

1   Heat the oil in a medium-size saucepan on medium to high heat. Sauté the onion slices for about 7 minutes until translucent and slightly golden.

2   Add the garlic and chicken livers and cook this for 5–7 minutes on high heat.

3   Adjust the heat to medium and stir in all the remaining ingredients. Cook, covered, for a further 10 minutes.

4   You can add a dash of water if you want the dish to be saucier, which makes it perfect for dipping bread into, ladling over warm noodles or rice, or leave it dry, which allows you to spread chunks of it on toast or crackers.

Braised
Chicken Livers
(page 81)

Braised Pilchards
(page 85)

Braised Tuna
(page 84)

comfort in minutes. You can choose to forego the potatoes to turn it into the perfect filling for closed sandwiches or as a topping for open sandwiches and crackers. My late father cooked this dish exceptionally well, and it was one that was often prepared for all his grandchildren when they were visiting. It was mostly served with rice, but when the grandkids were visiting, he'd often prepare fried potato chips with it and spoon the tuna sauce over them!

SERVES 4 | **PREPARATION TIME** 15 minutes | **COOKING TIME** 40 minutes

1 Tbsp (15 ml) canola or sunflower oil
1 medium-size onion, finely chopped
1 clove garlic, peeled and crushed
1 medium-size tomato, finely chopped
1 fresh green chilli, halved lengthwise
Salt to taste
1 tsp (5 ml) sugar
1 C (250 ml) water
2 medium-size potatoes, peeled and
    cubed into bite-size portions
2 cans (170 g each) tuna chunks in
    brine, drained
1 can (170 g) tuna chunks in oil, not drained
½ tsp (2.5 ml) freshly ground black pepper
Slices of fresh red chillies, for garnishing

1 Heat the oil in a saucepan on medium to high heat and add the chopped onion, garlic, tomato, chilli and salt.
2 Sauté for 5 minutes, stirring frequently, until the onion and tomato mixture is slightly browned.
3 Add the sugar and stir, then just as the onion and tomatoes are about to catch on the bottom of the saucepan, add 2–3 Tbsp (30–45 ml) of the water.
4 Add the potatoes and cook on high heat for about 2 minutes, then add the rest of the water. Reduce the heat to low and cook, covered, for 10–12 minutes or until the liquid has transformed into a lush sauce.
5 Place all the canned tuna on top of the potatoes – do not stir!
6 Cook, covered, on high heat for 3 minutes and then turn the heat down to medium for about 20 minutes, adding more water if needed.
7 Sprinkle the pepper generously over the tuna and now fold everything together. This is to ensure that the tuna and potatoes are well coated with sauce and that everything has come together.
8 Garnish with chilli slices and serve with fresh white bread or buns, seeded or health bread, basmati rice or on crackers.

Braised Pilchards
(Ouma Raggie's Pilchard Smoor)

The modest can of pilchards is deeply rooted in our South African heritage food narrative. Whether you grew up eating the Saldanha pilchards in tomato or the hot and spicy Lucky Star brand, it reminds all of us of our grandmother's cooking. My Ouma prepared this for us with bread that was used to mop up all that spicy tomato sauce. We'd also often have the leftovers on a sandwich for school lunch. Years later, when I hosted a Tupperware party at home, my Ouma's pilchard smoortjie became the topping on seeded loaf and French bread – it was a hit with everyone!

SERVES 6 | **PREPARATION TIME** 15 minutes | **COOKING TIME** 40 minutes

1 Tbsp (15 ml) canola or sunflower oil

1 medium-size onion, finely chopped

1 clove garlic, peeled and crushed

1 fresh green chilli, halved lengthwise

Salt to taste

½ tsp (2.5 ml) chilli powder or kokni masala

1 C (250 ml) water

2 medium-size potatoes, peeled and cubed into bite-size pieces

2 cans (400 g each) pilchards, bones removed (save the canned sauce, which will be added to the dish during the cooking process)

1 Tbsp (15 ml) white sugar

½ tsp (2.5 ml) freshly ground black pepper

Squeeze of lemon juice

Chopped fresh parsley or spring onions, for garnishing

1. Heat the oil in a saucepan on medium to high heat and add the chopped onion, garlic and chilli.
2. Sauté for 5 minutes, stirring frequently, until the onion and garlic are slightly browned.
3. Add the salt, chilli powder or masala and stir, and just as the onions are about to catch on the bottom of the saucepan, add 2–3 Tbsp (30–45 ml) of the water.
4. Add the potatoes and cook on high heat for about 2 minutes, then add the rest of the water. Reduce the heat to low and simmer gently for 10–12 minutes or until the liquid has transformed into a lush sauce.
5. Place the pilchards and the sauce on top of the potatoes – do not stir!
6. Cook, covered, on high heat for 5 minutes and then turn the heat down to medium for about 20 minutes, adding more water if needed.
7. Sprinkle the sugar, pepper and lemon juice over the pilchards, and now fold everything together to ensure that the pilchards and potatoes are well coated with sauce and that everything has come together.
8. Garnish with parsley or spring onions and serve with fresh white bread or buns, seeded or health bread, basmati rice or on crackers.

Spicy Tomato and Onion Relish
(Gesmore Tamatie)

This is the holy grail of smoortjies! It is not only the base of most smoortjies where a protein is later added, but on its own it serves as an accompaniment to main dishes such as masala fish, fried liver or frikkadel. It is so versatile that I use it as a pizza sauce by adding ingredients like tomato purée or paste, freshly ground pepper and Italian herbs. If you love French fries, slap chips or spuds, then add a few fragrant spices to transform it into a spicy chip drizzle or dip.

SERVES 6 | **PREPARATION TIME** 15 minutes | **COOKING TIME** 20 minutes

2 Tbsp (30 ml) olive, canola
  or sunflower oil
1 medium-size onion,
  finely chopped

4 large or 5–6 medium tomatoes,
  roughly chopped
1 clove garlic, peeled and crushed
1 fresh green chilli, finely chopped

Salt to taste
½ C (125 ml) white sugar
1 Tbsp (15 ml) tomato paste
½ C (125 ml) water

1 Heat the oil in a saucepan on medium to high heat and add the chopped onion, tomatoes, garlic, chilli and salt.
2 Sauté for 7–10 minutes, stirring frequently, until the onion and tomato mixture is lightly browned.
3 Add the sugar and tomato paste and stir, then just as the onion and tomatoes are about to catch on the bottom of the saucepan, add the water a little bit at a time.
4 Reduce the heat to low and simmer gently for 10–12 minutes or until the liquid has transformed into a lush and velvety sauce.
5 Serve alongside grilled fish or frikkadel (meatballs) or ladle over mashed potatoes or pap.

VARIATIONS
Chips Curry Dip or Drizzle

1 Tbsp (15 ml) canola or sunflower oil
1 small onion, finely chopped
2 large or 4 medium tomatoes, skinned
    and roughly chopped
1 clove garlic, peeled and crushed
½ green chilli, finely chopped
Salt to taste
1 Tbsp (15 ml) white sugar
1 Tbsp (15 ml) tomato paste
½ C (125 ml) water
2 tsp (10 ml) Pakco curry powder
1 tsp (5 ml) kokni masala or ½ tsp (2.5 ml)
    curry powder
1 tsp (5 ml) paprika
¼ tsp (1.25 ml) turmeric

1   Follow steps 1 to 4 of the Spicy Tomato
    and Onion Relish recipe (see opposite),
    adding the variation spices at the same
    time you add the sugar in step 3.
2   Drizzle over slap chips or use as a spicy
    dip for crispy French fries.

Pizza Base Sauce

1 Tbsp (15 ml) canola or sunflower oil
1 small onion, finely chopped
1 large or 2 medium tomatoes, skinned
    and roughly chopped
1 clove garlic, peeled and crushed
Salt to taste
1 Tbsp (15 ml) white sugar, or to taste
½ C (125 ml) tomato purée or 2 Tbsp (30 ml)
    tomato paste
½ C (125 ml) water
½ tsp (2.5 ml) freshly ground black pepper
1 Tbsp (15 ml) dried Italian herbs or
    ½ Tbsp (7.5 ml) dried oregano or thyme
¼ tsp (1.25 ml) dried chilli flakes or
    cayenne pepper (optional)

1 Follow steps 1 to 4 of the Spicy Tomato and Onion Relish recipe (page 86), adding the variation spices and herbs at the same time you add the sugar in step 3.
2 When done, allow the sauce to cool completely and then spread over pizza bases, toasted ciabatta or panini slices.

Rice with Braised Meat & Potatoes
(Rys Brensie)

Rys brensie is an aromatic one-pot-wonder consisting of braised meat and rice topped with deep-fried, golden potato wedges. The dish itself has very few ingredients but, like most rice dishes, requires a fair amount of patience and a watchful eye. The flavour of the dish is derived from the whole spices that are cooked with the meat and slices of onions. Note that these spices are removed before serving otherwise they give an unpleasant taste when bitten into. Slow cooking is advised to ensure that all that flavour from the caramelised onions and spices pervades and can be discerned when the rice and potatoes are added.

SERVES 6 | **PREPARATION TIME** 15 minutes | **COOKING TIME** 1 hour 15 minutes

1½ C (375 ml) basmati rice

2 Tbsp (30 ml) canola or sunflower oil

4 whole allspice

5 whole cloves

2 sticks cassia bark or cinnamon

2 cardamom pods, bruised

2 onions, thinly sliced

Salt to taste

700 g lamb pieces or stewing beef, bone in

3 C (750 ml) water

1 clove garlic, peeled and crushed

1 fresh green chilli

1 tsp (5 ml) freshly ground black pepper

½ tsp (2.5 ml) ground nutmeg

4 potatoes, peeled and sliced

Canola or vegetable oil, for deep-frying

1. Prepare the rice just slightly undercooked, drain and set aside until needed.
2. Heat the oil in a large saucepan on medium to high heat and add the allspice, whole cloves, cinnamon, cardamom pods and slices of onions. Cook for about 10 minutes, stirring frequently.
3. Season with salt and add the meat. Braise for 10 minutes.
4. Reduce the heat to medium, add 2 cups (500 ml) water and cook, covered, for 30–40 minutes until the sauce has reduced.
5. Add the garlic, green chilli, ground pepper and nutmeg and cook for about 5 minutes until fragrant.
6. Reduce the heat to low, add the remaining water and simmer gently for about 20 minutes.
7. In the meantime, deep-fry the potato slices and set aside until needed.
8. Scatter the cooked rice on top of the meat and gravy, add the fried potatoes and allow everything to heat through for about 5 minutes.
9. Turn off the stove and leave the saucepan on the stove top for 10 minutes before serving.

TRADITIONAL COMFORT FOOD WITH AN AIR-FRYER OR INSTANT POT TWIST

SLOW COOKING FAST TRACKED

When it comes to traditional Cape Malay heritage food, a few dishes spring to mind: denningvleis (the oldest dish in our repertoire), fragrant bobotie, an array of aromatic curries and our beloved bredies. Many of these dishes often require slow cooking and a watchful eye and therefore much of the younger generation of Cape Malays veers away from cooking it.

Though I am the eternal Cape Malay purist when it comes to heritage food, I can attest to the fact that both my Instant Pot and air-fryer have become my treasured 'helpers' in the kitchen, especially when I am pressed for time. I'll also be the first to admit that before using the Instant Pot pressure cooker, I had never used a pressure cooker before. Now that I am more seasoned, I would also like to dispel the notion that cooking with the Instant Pot is simply a matter of adding all the ingredients into the pot, selecting a setting, securing the lid and 30 minutes later, you'll have a deliciously, tender and flavourful meal!

My guidance to you is to view the Instant Pot as a pressure-cooking pot that has its own heating element and a few additional useful attachments. You'll still be required to spend some time in the kitchen using the machine and you'll be pleasantly surprised at how much it builds your confidence to cook and bake once you have it down to a fine art. I guess what I am saying is, both the Instant Pot and air-fryer are not hands-off appliances or devices – they still require a hands-on approach. Also note that the models I have are the Instant Pot Duo Series and Air-fryer Instant Vortex Plus.

Practice makes perfect, and I have become a better Instant Pot and air-fryer user only because of all my mishaps and burnt blunders! Apart from time spent watching YouTube tutorials, my dearest foodie friend Farzana Kumandan, the founder of food blog *Sprinkles and Spice*, is an absolute pro when it comes to using these appliances for cooking and baking. In addition to her food blog and teaching cooking and baking classes, she is also the editor and food writer for *The Voice* in Cape Town, where she shares recipes, tips and advice with her devoted followers.

She's inspired this chapter, as I took on the challenge of creating my own selection of traditional Cape Malay dishes, eagerly introducing them to my Instant Pot and air-fryer. Farzana's Leg of Lamb (page 96) has also become my staple for special Sunday lunches and for Eid feasts.

Here are some guidelines that I believe allowed me to gain my confidence using both my air-fryer and Instant Pot and now they have me hooked on making those traditional Cape Malay delicacies with minimal effort, at twice the speed and with oodles of tender, delicious goodness!

AIR-FRYER

Read the manual or watch a few tutorials – Your air-fryer's manual has a handy table of cooking times and temperatures for common foods. There are loads of tutorials on how to use your air-fryer and you'll be blown away by the glorious goodies you can conjure up in them.

Reheated food – Apart from cooking, one of the attributes that I love about the air-fryer is that it is terrific for reheating food and won't make once-crispy things soggy, which often happens with a microwave. This is like a turbo-toaster – your reheated food will come out crisper and piping hot.

It's hands-on – You'll need to remove the basket during the cooking phase and shuffle the food around a few times to ensure even browning and crisping.

Preheating – I prefer to preheat, though you don't have to. However, if you're starting food in a cold air-fryer, your cooking time will increase two- or three-fold.

Moderate temperatures – I use a slightly lower temperature because the air-fryer gets hot very quickly and the hot air circulates. Moderate temperatures assist in providing a more golden tinge to the dish and will create a crispy outer layer while cooking completely on the inside.

Food cooks faster with moderate quantities – The less food in the basket, the shorter the cooking time; the more food, the longer the cooking time. Therefore, I use smaller quantities, which means that the food cooks much faster than what I am used to. It's one of the best attributes of the air-fryer.

Use the grate in the basket – This allows hot air to circulate all around the food and prevents the food from cooking in excess oil.

Peek-a-boo – Don't be afraid to a have a little peek at any point during the cooking process. You won't be disturbing anything and there's no need to shut off the machine. Just pull out the drawer, have a peek, move the food around if you must and close the drawer. The air-fryer will automatically start up again. NB: Ensure that the drawer is pushed all the way in, otherwise it won't turn back on.

Frozen food items – With both the air-fryer and Instant Pot, you do not need to defrost frozen food before cooking. Though I don't like cooking with food that has not been defrosted, I was very excited to get an air-fryer for my son while he was still a student. It doesn't leave the frozen food soggy when cooked, like the microwave often does.

INSTANT POT

Size matters – The 3-quart is right for you if you're short on space and only cooking for one or two people. The 6-quart is the one I have, which allows me to cook for up to six people. The recipes in this cookbook have been created using the 6-quart Instant Pot. Make adjustments to your recipes if necessary to accommodate the size of your Instant Pot.

Use liquid – A pressure cooker uses steam to build pressure that ultimately cooks the food to perfection. To create that pressure, the inner pot must have at least ½–1 C (125–250 ml) liquid. This allows for the pressure to build up, steam to be created and prevents the food from being burnt.

Start with sauté setting and experiment with the multiple features when cooking – The sauté setting assists with caramelising onions and braising, browning and searing meat right at the start of the cooking process. Switch to the pressure-cooking setting when it's time to add the remaining ingredients. It's also convenient to leave the food in the Instant Pot once it's been cooked – this way it stays cocooned in the heat for much longer. Alternatively, you can also use the warming function, which will keep your food warm until you're ready to serve.

The process does take time – The Instant Pot takes about 10 minutes to build the necessary pressure within the inner pot. If you are going to use the pressure cook buttons, you'll want to add 10–15 minutes cooking time to let the unit sufficiently pressurise. This means the cooking process only starts after the 10 or 15 minutes.

Beat the bland – It's evident that much as the Instant Pot locks in flavour and moisture, it does require a good amount of seasoning. I am inclined to add more salt, seasoning and/or aromatics than I would with traditional, stovetop cooking.

Adjust the temperature – I encourage you to adjust the temperature when using the sauté or slow-cooker functions. This helps you get the perfect cooking temperature specific to whatever dish you're making. Some dishes may need a slightly higher temperature, while you may want to turn down the heat on other dishes.

Sauce or gravy vs watery liquid – The Instant Pot retains liquid really well, which means it could negatively impact a dish that requires a thick and lush gravy versus a watery sauce. You may need to thicken the sauce by using a thickener like cornflour or plain flour, because cooking the dish further might ruin it. A word of caution though: add the thickener after the cooking process and use the sauté setting without the lid. This way you can control the consistency.

Frequently clean the nooks and crannies – The rim of an Instant Pot (where the lid sits) can accumulate dirt after a few uses. Sauce and juices can build up, making your pot look and smell gross. Wipe out all the nooks and crannies after each use to keep the pot looking and functioning at its best. I also invert the lid after cleaning, so that the top of the lid is facing downward and resting on the pot. This way everything is aerated to prevent bacteria from forming in moist spots and creating a musty smell.

Farzana's Legendary Leg of Lamb

This is certainly a much faster and less tedious way of preparing leg of lamb compared to the traditional way, which is to parboil the leg of lamb and then slow-cook it on the stove top. Farzana shares her recipe for Eid leg of lamb, which starts off the cooking process in the Instant Pot before being roasted in the oven and drizzled with a lush gravy before serving. She has her own blend of aromatics, but in the absence of that you can easily just add salt, dried chilli flakes and pepper, and you'll still have a lovely, seasoned leg of lamb.

SERVES 6–8 | **PREPARATION TIME** 30 minutes | **COOKING TIME** 1 hour 30 minutes

FOR THE GRAVY SLURRY

½ C (125 ml) cold or tepid water

2 Tbsp (30 ml) cornflour

½ tsp (2.5 ml) freshly ground black pepper

¼ tsp (1.25 ml) salt

FOR THE LEG OF LAMB

2 Tbsp (30 ml) olive oil, depending on the amount of fat on the meat

1 tsp (5 ml) freshly ground black pepper

¼ tsp (1.25 ml) fine black or white pepper

1 Tbsp (15 ml) lemon pepper

1 tsp (5 ml) dried chilli flakes

Salt to taste

1 leg of lamb, prepared by your butcher to fit your Instant Pot, or deboned

50 g butter

4 cloves garlic, peeled and bruised

6–8 baby potatoes, washed but unpeeled

6–8 shallots or medium-size pickling onions

4 carrots, peeled and cut into portions the same size as the baby potatoes

¾ C (200 ml) water

3 sprigs fresh rosemary

PREPARING THE GRAVY SLURRY

1   Place all the gravy ingredients into a jug and whisk to form a smooth slurry. Set aside until the lamb has been cooked.

PREPARING THE LEG OF LAMB

1   Place the olive oil, spices and salt in a small bowl and mix together. Set aside.

2   Dab the leg of lamb with paper towel to remove the excess moisture. This will allow the oil and spices to adhere to the lamb.

3   Rub the aromatics and oil mixture all over the lamb and into the crevices.

4   Place the lamb onto a roasting tray, which you'll use throughout the cooking process. Cover with plastic wrap and allow to come to room temperature before cooking.

5   You won't need the lid of the Instant Pot during the first phase of the cooking process. Set the Instant Pot to the Sauté setting on high, which means you'll press sauté three times.

6   Add the butter and, once it's melted, add the leg of lamb.

7   Sear the lamb for about 5 minutes on each side until it develops sear marks or has a deep golden colour.

8   Press cancel on the Instant Pot and transfer the lamb to the same roasting tray.

9. Place the garlic cloves, potatoes, shallots and carrots into the Instant Pot. Use the Sauté setting on high and sauté the vegetables, stirring frequently.
10. Add the water and bring to a boil, still uncovered, and simmer for 1 minute. This assists with deglazing the pot and is a crucial step to avoid burning.
11. Spread out the vegetables and place the seared lamb directly on top of them.
12. Cancel the Sauté setting and secure the lid of the Instant Pot.
13. Move the vent up to the Sealing Position. Select the Pressure Cook setting and select high pressure for 35 minutes.
14. Once done, allow the pressure to release naturally, i.e. wait for the pin to drop.
15. In the meantime, preheat the oven to 220 ºC.
16. When the pressure has released, transfer the leg of lamb and the potatoes back to the roasting tray.
17. Leave half the onions and one carrot portion in the pot. Arrange the rest of the vegetables around the lamb and potatoes and tuck in the sprigs of rosemary.
18. If the meat doesn't contain too much fat, drizzle about 2 Tbsp (30 ml) olive oil over the lamb and vegetables.
19. Roast in the oven for about 20 minutes or until golden.
20. In the meantime, set the Instant Pot to Sauté mode and use a masher (or stick blender) to mash the remaining ingredients into a smooth consistency.
21. Using a whisk, add the prepared gravy slurry, and give this a good mix. Switch off the Instant Pot.
22. Transfer the gravy from the inner pot of the Instant Pot and pour it through a sieve into a large bowl, pushing all the remnants of the gravy through with the back of a spoon.
23. Remove the leg of lamb and vegetables from the oven and pour over the gravy. Serve warm.

My Instant Pot Biryani

Once I got this recipe down to a T, I realised that I would not want to make biryani and even akni any other way! The potatoes are like little cloud puffs, tender and fluffy and the meat falls off the bone – a result of pressure cooking! This recipe doesn't even require you to marinate the meat overnight because the flavour permeates throughout all the ingredients, including the meat.

SERVES 6–8 | **PREPARATION TIME** 30 minutes | **COOKING TIME** 1 hour 15 minutes

FOR THE YOGHURT MARINADE

1 C (250 ml) plain yoghurt or buttermilk
   or amasi
2 Tbsp (30 ml) garlic and ginger paste
2 Tbsp (30 ml) biryani masala
1 Tbsp (15 ml) garam masala
1 tsp (5 m) Kashmiri chilli powder or
   Pakco roasted masala
½ tsp (2.5 ml) turmeric
1 Tbsp (15 ml) ground cumin
½ tsp (2.5 ml) saffron threads
2 tsp (10 ml) salt
1 ripe tomato, skinned and grated
1 fresh green chilli,
   split lengthwise

PREPARING THE MARINADE WITH THE MEAT

1 Dab the leg of lamb with paper towel to remove all the excess moisture. This allows the marinade to adhere to the lamb.
2 Mix all the marinade ingredients together in a bowl. Add the portions of meat and mix well. Cover with plastic wrap and set aside.

(Continued overleaf)

FOR THE BIRYANI

700 g shoulder or leg of lamb portions, bone in

½ C (125 ml) canola or vegetable oil

3 potatoes, peeled and halved or quartered, patted dry with a kitchen towel

3 onions, thinly sliced

2 cardamom pods, slightly bruised

2 cinnamon sticks

2 bay leaves

3½ C (875 ml) water

2 C (500 ml) basmati rice, rinsed until the water runs clear, drained

½ C (125 ml) brown lentils, cooked in 2 C (500 ml) water for 10 minutes, rinsed and drained , or canned lentils, rinsed and drained

Salt to taste

50 g butter

4–6 hard-boiled eggs

10 strands saffron threads, soaked in 2 Tbsp (30 ml) warm water

PREPARING THE BIRYANI

1 You won't need the lid of the Instant Pot during the first phase of the cooking process. Set the Instant Pot to the Sauté setting on high, which means you'll press sauté three times.

2 Add the oil and then, once the oil is warm, add the potatoes and fry until golden and crisp on the outside but not yet cooked on the inside. Remove with a slotted spoon and set aside in a bowl.

3 Add the onions and fry for 15–20 minutes or until the onions are golden. Remove half of the onions with a slotted spoon and set aside in a bowl.

4 Press cancel on the Instant Pot. Add the meat and yoghurt marinade, the cardamom, cinnamon and bay leaves, and ½ C (125 ml) water to the Instant Pot.

5 Move the vent to the Sealing Position. Select the pressure cook setting and cook on high pressure for 25 minutes.

6 Once done, allow the pressure to release naturally, i.e. wait for the pin to drop.

7 When the pressure is released, place the partially fried potatoes in between the meat, then add half the rinsed rice, ensuring that you spread out the rice to cover the meat and potatoes.

8 Cover the rice with a layer of brown lentils. At this stage I also sprinkle 1 tsp (5 ml) salt over the lentils.

9 Add the remaining rice and spread this out over the lentils.

10 Add the remaining 3 C (750 ml) water and secure the lid.

11 Move the vent up to Sealing Position. Push Meat/Stew on Medium Pressure and set the time to 7 minutes.

12 Once done, allow the pressure to release naturally, i.e. wait for the pin to drop.

13 When the pressure is released, dot the partially cooked breyani with cubes of butter, pushing it down into the rice, ever so gently. Do the same with the hard-boiled eggs. Pour the saffron strands and water over the rice and eggs.

14 Secure the lid of the Instant Pot again and move the vent up to Sealing Position. Allow the biryani to rest for about 20 minutes until the rice has puffed up.

15 To serve, I remove the inner pot of the Instant Pot and set it down on the kitchen table surface. Place a large serving platter or large bowl over the inner pot and upend it.

16 Allow it to stand like this for about 2 minutes, then gently lift the inner pot to expose the different layers of the biryani.

17 Remove any leftovers from the inner pot, add it to the rest of the biryani and serve with Tomato and Onion Relish (page 189).

Bobotie Royale

The Instant Pot is perfect for this recipe because it locks in flavour and keeps the bobotie moist. It also creates a feathery light egg custard topping – the pot doesn't crisp up the topping so I pop it into the air-fryer for 3–5 minutes to attain that golden blush on the top. If I am really pressed for time a chef's blowtorch does the trick as well. The easiest way to prepare this is using a springform baking tin – it works well with both the air-fryer and Instant Pot, and the two colourful layers are beautifully presented when served.

SERVES 6–8 | **PREPARATION TIME** 30 minutes | **COOKING TIME** 20 minutes

FOR THE EGG CUSTARD
4 large eggs, beaten
1 C (250 ml) milk
1 tsp (5 ml) freshly grated nutmeg
Pinch of salt

FOR THE BOBOTIE
600 g lamb or beef mince
1 egg, beaten
4 slices stale bread, crusts removed, soaked
   in 1 C (250 ml) water for 5 minutes, drained
2 Tbsp (30 ml) canola, sunflower or olive oil
2 medium-size onions, finely sliced
2 tsp (10 ml) salt, or to taste
1 clove garlic, peeled and crushed
1 tsp (5 ml) turmeric
¼ tsp (1.25 ml) ground cloves (optional)
2 tsp (10 ml) Pakco curry powder
1 tsp (5 ml) kokni masala or ½ tsp (2.5 ml)
   chilli powder
¼ C (60 ml) golden sultanas or dried
   cranberries, soaked in ½ C (125 ml) cooled
   boiling water for 5 minutes, then drained
5 dried Turkish apricots, thinly sliced
4 bay leaves or citrus leaves, for garnishing

PREPARING THE EGG CUSTARD
1 Place all the ingredients into a mixing bowl and whisk. Set aside.

PREPARING THE BOBOTIE
1 Prepare a 20 cm springform pan by spraying it with nonstick spray. Also line the outside of the pan with aluminium foil to ensure it doesn't leak during cooking.
2 Place the mince, beaten egg and bread (excess water squeezed out) into a mixing bowl. Use your hands to mix together until it resembles a meatloaf consistency. Set aside.
3 Turn on the Instant Pot and set it to Sauté mode on high setting. Heat the oil and then add the sliced onions.
4 Sauté the onions for 10 minutes, stirring every now and again.
5 Add the salt, garlic, turmeric, ground cloves (if using) and curry powder, masala or chilli powder and sauté for 2 minutes, adding just a dash of water if the ingredients are sticking to the bottom of the pot.
6 Switch off the Instant Pot and transfer the warm ingredients to the meatloaf mixture.
7 Add the soaked sultanas and sliced apricots and use a wooden spoon to combine.

8 The next step is to cook the bobotie, which means you'll have to wash the inner pot of the Instant Pot first. Once washed, rinsed and dried, place it back into the Instant Pot 'casing'.

9 Place the steaming rack into the Instant Pot.

10 Pour ¼ C (60 ml) water into the Instant Pot.

11 Spoon the mince mixture into the prepared springform tin and smooth the top.

12 Place the springform tin on top of the steaming rack.

13 Pour the egg custard layer on top and garnish with the bay or citrus leaves.

14 Secure the lid and move the vent up to Sealing Position. Select Meat/Stew on Medium Pressure and set the time to 10 minutes.

15 Once done, allow the pressure to release naturally, i.e. wait for the pin to drop.

16 Unlock and open the lid. Remove the springform tin and transfer to the air-fryer.

17 Set the air-fryer to 200 ºC and air-fry for 4–6 minutes or until golden on top.

18 Remove the pan gently and rest on a cooling rack.

19 Insert a knife between the bobotie and springform pan and run it along the edges of the bobotie. Open the latch of the springform pan and extend the latch so that the sides of the pan separate from the bobotie.

20 Lift the bobotie with an egg lifter or slide it onto a serving platter.

21 Serve with a leafy salad.

Cape Malay Sago Bredie
Inspired by the late Faldela Williams

I draw on the late Faldela Williams for this dish from her book *The Cape Malay Cookbook*. She maintained that this bredie 'is a traditional bredie and popular with the old folk who find it easy to digest'.

SERVES 6 | **PREPARATION TIME** 30 minutes | **COOKING TIME** 1 hour

2 Tbsp (30 ml) canola, sunflower
  or olive oil
2 medium-size onions, very finely chopped
700 g lamb knuckles
½ C (125 ml) water
5 whole cloves
5 whole allspice
1 tsp (5 ml) freshly ground black pepper
½ tsp (2.5 ml) grated nutmeg
Salt to taste
1 clove garlic, peeled and crushed
½ C (125 ml) sago, soaked in 1 C (250 ml)
  water for 30 minutes
2 Tbsp (30 ml) finely chopped fresh
  flat-leaf parsley

1 Turn on the Instant Pot and set it to Sauté mode on high setting. Heat the oil, then add the onions and sauté for 5–7 minutes or until the onions are translucent and slightly golden.
2 Add lamb knuckles and give everything a good stir. Sauté for 5 minutes.
3 Add the water and select Cancel to switch off Sauté mode.
4 At this point, spread out the meat to ensure that it cooks evenly.
5 Secure the lid and move the vent up to Sealing Position. Push Meat/Stew on High Pressure and set the time to 15 minutes.
6 Once done, allow the pressure to release naturally, i.e. wait for the pin to drop.
7 Remove the lid and set the Instant Pot to Sauté setting medium (normal). Add all the aromatics (spices), including the salt and crushed garlic. Sauté for 7 minutes.
8 Add the sago and 1 Tbsp (15 ml) of the chopped parsley and give this a good stir with the rest of the ingredients.
9 Secure the lid and move the vent up to Sealing Position. Push Meat/Stew on High Pressure and set the time to 15 minutes.
10 Once done, allow the pressure to release naturally, i.e. wait for the pin to drop.
11 When the pressure is released, garnish with the remaining chopped parsley and serve in a bowl or ladle the sago bredie over mashed potatoes.

Cape Malay Lamb Curry
on a Fluffy Mound of Couscous

Cape Malay curries are all about depth of flavour and moderate heat. The sauce for the curry is derived from the tomatoes and if you don't have ripe and sweet tomatoes, then the canned Italian plum tomatoes will do. I like to use a combination of fresh and canned tomatoes – together these provide a deeper colour to the curry and a velvety gravy. I've also included variations on page 113 to give you the freedom to make a meat, chicken or vegetable curry using the same curry sauce.

SERVES 6 | **PREPARATION TIME** 30 minutes | **COOKING TIME** 40 minutes

FOR THE CURRY SAUCE

1 large, fresh and ripe tomato, skinned and halved
½ can (200 g) whole Italian tomatoes, skins removed
1 fresh green chilli
4–6 fresh curry leaves
2 sprigs fresh coriander
1 tsp (5 ml) turmeric
2 tsp (10 ml) ground cumin
2 tsp (10 ml) Pakco curry powder or roasted masala
1 tsp (5 ml) kokni masala or ½ tsp (2.5 ml) chilli powder
2 Tbsp (30 ml) white sugar
1 tsp (5 ml) salt

FOR THE COUSCOUS

2 C (500 ml) couscous
1 tsp (5 ml) salt, or to taste
2 Tbsp (30 ml) canola oil or olive oil
3 ½ C (875 ml) boiling water

PREPARING THE CURRY SAUCE

1   Place both the fresh and canned tomatoes, green chilli, curry leaves and sprigs of coriander into a food processor and pulse three to four times.
2   Add the remaining sauce ingredients and pulse until it forms a smooth sauce. Set aside.
3   If you're not making the curry right away, the curry sauce can be stored in an airtight container in the refrigerator for up to five days or in the freezer for up to three months.

PREPARING THE COUSCOUS

1   Place the couscous, salt, oil and boiling water into a large bowl.
2   Immediately cover the bowl with plastic wrap and set aside until the couscous has doubled in size.
3   Use a fork to fluff the couscous just before serving.

FOR THE LAMB CURRY

2 Tbsp (30 ml) canola or sunflower oil
1 cinnamon stick
2 cardamom pods, slightly bruised
1 onion, finely chopped
1 Tbsp (15 ml) garlic and ginger paste
    or ½ thumb-size portion fresh ginger,
    peeled and grated, and 2 cloves garlic,
    peeled and crushed
700 g leg of lamb, bone in, cut into
    stewing portions
½ C (125 ml) water
3 medium-size potatoes, peeled and
    halved or 6–8 baby potatoes,
    washed with skins on
Salt to taste

PREPARING THE LAMB CURRY

1 Turn on the Instant Pot and set it to Sauté mode on high setting. Heat the oil, then add the whole spices, chopped onion and garlic and ginger.

2 Sauté the ingredients for about 5 minutes, stirring every now and again.

3 Add the lamb portions and give everything a good stir. Sauté for 5 minutes.

4 Add the water and select Cancel to switch off Sauté mode.

5 At this point, evenly spread out the meat to ensure that it cooks evenly.

6 Secure the lid and move the vent up to Sealing Position. Push Meat/Stew on High Pressure and set the time to 15 minutes.

7 Once done, allow the pressure to release naturally, i.e. wait for the pin to drop.

8 Unlock and open the lid and add the potatoes to the cooked meat.

9 Pour the prepared curry sauce over the meat and potatoes.

10 At this stage, you have to make a judgement call. If the sauce looks too runny, which means the potatoes and meat are halfway covered in liquid, then don't add any additional water. If the liquid seems too little, you can add ¼ C (60 ml) water.

11 Secure the lid again and move the vent up to Sealing Position. Select Meat/Stew on High Pressure and set the time to 10 minutes.

12 Once done, allow the pressure to release naturally, i.e. wait for the pin to drop.

13 Serve in individual bowls, spooned on top of a golden mound of fluffy couscous.

Serves 4

Baby Marrow Carrots and
Gem Squash Curry (Okra)

1 dozen mid...
1 bunch
2 very
1 onio
3 tb
2 sl
10 m
5 ml
4½ m
1 s

VARIATIONS

VEGETABLE CURRY: Follow the same steps as the lamb curry on page 111, but in step 3 add 700 g vegetables of choice and give everything a good stir. Sauté for 3 minutes, stirring frequently. Then, in step 6, secure the lid and move the vent up to Sealing Position. Select Meat/Stew on High Pressure and set the time to 7 minutes. Once done, allow the pressure to release naturally, i.e. wait for the pin to drop.

MINCE CURRY: Follow the same steps as the lamb curry on page 111, but in step 3 add 700 g beef or lamb mince and give everything a good stir. Skip to step 6, but add all the remaining ingredients. Secure the lid and move the vent up to Sealing Position. Select Meat/Stew on High Pressure and set the time to 10 minutes. Once done, allow the pressure to release naturally, i.e. wait for the pin to drop.

CHICKEN CURRY: Follow the same steps as the lamb curry on page 111, but in step 3 add 1 kg chicken portions and give everything a good stir. Sauté for 5 minutes, stirring frequently. Skip to step 6, but add all the remaining ingredients. Secure the lid and move the vent up to Sealing Position. Select Meat/Stew on High Pressure and set the time to 10 minutes. Once done, allow the pressure to release naturally, i.e. wait for the pin to drop.

CRAYFISH OR PRAWN CURRY: Follow steps 1 and 2 of the lamb curry on page 111. Ignore steps 3–8. Then, in step 9, add the curry sauce and cook on Sauté mode for 10 minutes, stirring frequently. Ignore all other steps. You can either submerge your cooked crayfish (page 120) into the sauce and give this a good toss, while sautéing for about 5 minutes, or drizzle the sauce over the crayfish and serve right away.

Cape Malay Denningvleis

One of the oldest dishes in the Cape Malay recipe vault is denningvleis and it's a perfect representation of the spices and flavours that are indicative of the flavours from the homelands of our forefathers. The traditional version has tender cuts of lamb marinated in a tamarind-based sauce, infused with subtle tones of allspice, bay leaf, cinnamon and cardamom, and a distinctive sweet and tangy gravy. In my version I use vinegar and the result is no different to the original recipe. It is served with sweet yellow rice, mashed potatoes and steamed vegetables, coated with glistening warm butter and a generous dusting of nutmeg.

SERVES 6 | **PREPARATION TIME** 30 minutes | **COOKING TIME** 1 hour

2 Tbsp (30 ml) vegetable or canola oil

2 large onions, finely chopped

1 tsp (5 ml) dried chilli flakes

½ tsp (2.5 ml) freshly ground black pepper

5 whole allspice

1 kg leg of lamb, bone in, cut into cubes

1 tsp (5 ml) salt

1 Tbsp (15 ml) white sugar or to taste

4 cloves garlic, peeled and crushed

3 large bay leaves

2 Tbsp (30 ml) brown vinegar

1 C (250 ml) water

1 It is crucial that the meat is seared and braised well, which means it must have that terracotta-coloured appearance indicative of a deep-coloured Malaysian and Indonesian beef rendang.

2 Turn on the Instant Pot and set it to Sauté mode on high setting. Heat the oil, then add the onions, chilli flakes, pepper and allspice and sauté for 5–7 minutes or until the onions are translucent and slightly golden.

3 Add the lamb, salt, sugar, garlic and bay leaves and sauté for 10–15 minutes, searing the meat and browning it evenly.

4 Add the vinegar and cook on sauté mode for 5 minutes.

5 Add the water and select Cancel to switch off Sauté mode.

6 At this point, spread out the meat to ensure that it cooks evenly.

7 Secure the lid and move the vent up to Sealing Position. Select Meat/Stew on High Pressure and set the time to 20 minutes.

8 Once done, allow the pressure to release naturally, i.e. wait for the pin to drop.

9 Serve with fluffy rice or mashed potatoes.

BBQ Chicken Thighs and Drumsticks

This BBQ spice concoction is one that I love preparing for braais. It's zesty and spicy, and the addition of Mrs Ball's Chutney cuts through the lemony tinge and provides that sweet and tangy flavour profile that Cape Malays love. You can also easily substitute the chutney with apricot or peach jam or even caramelised onion chutney.

SERVES 6 | **PREPARATION TIME** 30 minutes | **COOKING TIME** 30 minutes

10 mixed portions of chicken thighs and drumsticks
¼ C (60 ml) plain yoghurt
2 Tbsp (30 ml) barbecue marinade (I've used Amina's Wonderspice Sweet Barbeque Marinade)
½ Tbsp (7.5 ml) braai spice (I've used Ina Paarman's Braai & Grill Seasoning)
½ Tbsp (7.5 ml) lemon pepper
2 Tbsp (30 ml) Mrs Ball's Chutney
¼ C (60 ml) barbecue sauce (I've used Ina Paarman's Sticky Marinade)
½ tsp (2.5 ml) dried chilli flakes (optional)
Salt to taste
½ C (125 ml) pomegranate jewels, for garnishing
½ C (125 ml) micro greens and/or sprigs of rosemary, for garnishing

1   Pat the chicken portions dry with paper towel to ensure that all the excess moisture is removed. This will allow the marinade and spices to adhere to the chicken.
2   Place all the ingredients, except the garnish, into a large bowl and mix until the chicken is well coated. Don't discard the marinade. You can use this to baste the chicken during the cooking process.
3   Arrange the chicken portions in the air-fryer basket in a single layer. Ensure that you start the thighs with the skin side facing up.
4   Cook at a temperature of 180 ºC for 15 minutes.
5   Open the drawer and flip over the portions. Use a basting or pastry brush to baste and coat the chicken with some of the reserved marinade.
6   Close the drawer and cook for another 10–15 minutes.
7   Open the drawer again and flip the chicken once more so that the skin side is facing up again, and brush all sides of the chicken with the remaining marinade. Air-fry for an additional 4 minutes.
8   Place all the chicken on a serving platter and garnish with pomegranate jewels and sprigs of rosemary and/or micro greens. Serve hot with grilled corn, or at room temperature or cold.

CARIEMA'S TIP

You may need to cook the chicken in two batches, depending on the portion sizes of the chicken.
If this is the case, preheat the oven to 180 ºC (later adjust the heat to 100 ºC) and when the first batch is done, it can be kept warm in the oven while you prepare the second batch.

Raziya's Yoghurt Masala Lamb Chops

My best friend, Raziya Salie, is always looking for quick and easy recipes with minimal effort but that are big on flavour. Her meat of choice is beef and for her and her husband Adenaan, a tender cut of rib-eye or sirloin is the remedy for all their carnivorous cravings. Raziya will be the first to tell me that she's not keen on lamb chops and yet, when I make this marinade and coat the lamb chops, she's also the first to enquire when dinner will be served!

FOR THE YOGHURT MARINADE

½ Tbsp (7.5 ml) lemon pepper
½ tsp (2.5 ml) freshly ground black pepper
½ tsp (2.5 ml) dried chilli flakes
1 tsp (2.5 ml) Amina's Wonderspice Steak
   and Chops marinade
¼ C (60 ml) plain yoghurt
1 Tbsp (15 ml) Mrs Ball's Chutney

FOR THE GARLIC, LEMON AND HERB-
INFUSED BUTTER BASTING SAUCE

50 g butter
1 clove garlic, crushed
Juice of ½ small lemon
2–3 sprigs fresh thyme or rosemary

FOR THE LAMB CHOPS

8 lamb chops
¼ C (60 ml) flat-leaf parsley, roughly
   chopped, for garnishing

PREPARING THE MARINADE

1 Place all the ingredients for the marinade into a mixing
   bowl and mix well.

PREPARING THE BUTTER BASTING SAUCE

1 Melt the butter in a small saucepan on low to
   medium heat.
2 Add the garlic and lemon juice. Allow to infuse
   for 2–3 minutes.
3 Switch off the stove and stir the herbs into the melted
   butter. Set aside.

LAMB CHOPS

1 Place the lamb chops into the marinade and massage
   this mixture into the meat until all the lamb chops are
   coated. Cover with plastic wrap and set aside for 1 hour
   or overnight.
2 Set the air-fryer at 180 °C and preheat it. Place the
   marinated chops into the basket and cook for 10 minutes.
   Open the drawer to the air-fryer after 2–3 minutes to flip
   the chops and brush them with the butter basting sauce.
3 Once done, adjust the air-fryer to the grill function and
   grill the chops for about 2 minutes.
4 Transfer the chops to a serving platter and brush with
   the remaining butter basting sauce. Garnish with fresh
   parsley and serve with flatbreads and a drizzle of yoghurt.

VARIATION

You can make this recipe using 4–6 rib-eye or sirloin steaks
instead of the lamb chops.

Tandoori Crayfish
with a Curry Sauce

Seafood, especially shellfish, is so easy to cook in an air-fryer. This recipe is great on its own or can be served with a curry sauce (page 110).

SERVES 6 | **PREPARATION TIME** 30 minutes | **COOKING TIME** 20 minutes

FOR THE MARINADE

2 cloves garlic, peeled and crushed

2 tsp (10 ml) seafood masala or
   curry powder

1 tsp (5 ml) Kashmiri chilli powder or
   spicy paprika

½ tsp (2.5 ml) freshly ground black pepper

1 tsp (5 ml) tomato paste

¼ C (60 ml) plain yoghurt

Salt to taste

FOR THE CRAYFISH

1 whole crayfish (ethically sourced), cut
   in half lengthwise and cleaned

8 crayfish tails (ethically sourced), cut
   in half lengthwise

Chopped fresh flat-leaf parsley and lime
   and/or lemon wedges, for garnishing

PREPARING THE MARINADE

1 Place all the ingredients for the marinade into a mixing bowl and mix well.

PREPARING THE CRAYFISH

1 Using a pastry brush, coat the shellfish with the marinade, then set aside on a baking tray for about 15 minutes.

2 Set the air-fryer at 180 °C and preheat it. Place the marinated shellfish into the basket and cook for 10 minutes. Open the drawer to the air-fryer after 2–3 minutes to flip and baste the shellfish with some of the marinade.

3 Once done, adjust the air-fryer to the grill function and grill the crayfish for about 2 minutes.

4 Transfer the crayfish to a serving platter and brush with the remaining marinade or drizzle with the curry sauce from page 110. Scatter over the parsley and add a squeeze of lime or lemon juice. Serve on a bed of rice with lime and/or lemon wedges on the side.

TOGETHER AS ONE

AGE-OLD TRADITIONS PRESERVED
IN AN EVER-CHANGING WORLD

My desire to keep my Cape Malay heritage relevant seems more meaningful now than ever before due to the impact of the Covid-19 pandemic. The negative affect on global economies has resulted in a downward spiral and for the better part of 2020 and 2021 we were all just hoping (and praying) that things would start looking up. Isolation and (physical) social distancing became the norm, altering our social activities and forcing us to become more remote than ever before. The only choice we had to stay safe was to stay home and to connect in a virtual environment.

Never had social media been more relevant than during the pandemic. It provided a constructive platform for us to share our daily experiences and stories. On the days that truly mattered, such as Easter, Christmas, Eid, Dewali, birthdays and anniversaries, we saw images of celebrations and the food that accompanied them. It was no different in the Islamic world as we kicked off the holy month of Ramadan. I observed a flood of foodie images and recipes being shared amongst Muslim food bloggers, home cooks, influencers and even novice cooks, across the world. This enticed many of us to try out new recipes, to have the courage to enter the kitchen domain and to prepare delicious treats to accompany some of our more traditional delicacies for our Ramadan iftar meals.

However, the religious celebrations that continue to take my breath away year upon year are Eid al-Fitr and Eid al-Adha, which seem to light up social media. Images are shared of families dressed in their finest attire, and Eid heritage food and delectable cakes and bakes adorning Eid tables, as we satisfy our savoury and sweet cravings after an arduous month of fasting. It is also for this reason that this chapter holds a special place in my heart as I commemorate these two momentous religious festivals – Ramadan and Eid – in the Islamic calendar.

These days we see a harmonious amalgamation of old and new in our Cape Malay community. We haven't abandoned our traditions; we remain devoted, but we have realised that change is part of life. In the culinary sphere, we have become bolder in our food choices: pairing heritage fare with new culinary additions, and shaking up legacy recipes with a modern twist.

We have also come to embrace the idea that the hours spent in the kitchen, cooking and baking for Eid, can simply be substituted by outsourcing. Purchasing from local suppliers, retail and home industries is all the rage. We have embraced the change without sacrificing our traditions. We've discovered that we can be devoted to both and that the two can co-exist in harmony. These types of celebrations are a representation not only of our community's transformation, but also signify that nothing is as powerful as the coming together of human beings. The very best of our characters emerge, our egos silenced by the need to be part of something much bigger than ourselves. We aspire to be kinder to each other on days like Eid and during Ramadan, and we yearn for the peace and calm it brings with it. The essence of our human spirit illuminates our homes as we welcome our guests to our tables. Our love language is clear as dishes are passed on from one person to another, the act of breaking bread together is set in motion. We are also more inclined to accept that these are some of the most unforgettable memories we are creating – when we come together as one!

Ramadan

Ramadan is the ninth month of the Islamic calendar and is observed by Muslims worldwide as a month of fasting, prayer, reflection and community or charity. It is also deemed the most auspicious month in the Islamic lunar calendar. Thus, fasting Muslims are inclined to embark on a spiritual rejuvenation by reciting the holy Quran and remaining devoted to prayers during this month. Additionally, a physical cleanse (a detox if you will) is incited, as we abstain from eating and drinking from sunrise to sunset. While food and drink become non-existent during the fasting hours, the antidote to this kind of abstinence is indeed prayer, reflection and a deeper consciousness into the lives of those who are far less fortunate than us.

For many Muslims across the world, Ramadan brings with it its own allure because the traditions associated with this month are often traditions that have been inculcated in us from an early age. For me, the Ramadans spent in Bo-Kaap remain the most vivid of my food memories as I reminisce about Ramadan koekies such as pancakes filled with sweet, fragrant coconut; spicy daltjies; samoosas and pumpkin fritters sprinkled with aromatic cinnamon sugar. As a child I'd get ready to go and deliver plates of koekies that my grandmother and mom would prepare to share with our neighbours. I would walk from door to door, one neighbour's house to another, and deliver my plate of koekies. I'd wait patiently as the 'Aunty' would disappear into her kitchen and exchange our koekies with hers.

My inspiration for the Ramadan fragment of this chapter is Feriel Sonday, who was born in District Six in the mid-1960s and, as the eldest daughter, she assisted her mom Fatima Sonday in the kitchen. Ferial accredits her culinary skill to the heart of their home, the kitchen, where she was introduced to a wonderful fusion of Indian, Cape Malay and traditional South African delights. After watching the Mexican film *Like Water for Chocolate*, which depicted an enchanted connection between food and feeling, Ferial was inspired to start her own food business from home. She became well known for her chocolate cakes that were described by customers as 'light as soufflés'. This popularity spurred her on to create her successful Facebook page called Feriel Sonday's Heavenly Bites, where she shares her fuss-free recipes with her devoted followers. She's pretty

hands on when it comes to answering questions about cooking and food preparation.

One of her other attributes that draws me even closer to her, is her kindness and generosity, which is very prevalent when you get to know her. She's a shining example of 'Cooking being a form of charity' – you'll often find her involved in community feeding schemes or sharing her recipes so freely, with her only intention being that you have success in cooking and baking, and that you enjoy every morsel with your friends and family.

Quick and Easy
Veggie Soup
(page 131)

Chicken Gyoza
Dumplings
(page 132)

Vietnamese-style Cold
Spring Rolls (page 133)

Sweet and
Savoury Dates
(page 129)

Peppered Steak Hand Pies
(page 134)

Quick and Easy Falooda Milkshake
(page 128)

Cape Malay Boeber
(page 130)

Quick and Easy Falooda Milkshake

There are many versions of falooda, some fancier than others. Mine is a simple rose flavoured milkshake that my father made for us when we were kids. It's topped with a scoop of creamy vanilla ice cream and garnished with tiny morsels of Turkish delight. For added bliss, top with whipped cream and a drizzle of crimson rose-flavoured syrup.

SERVES 4 | **PREPARATION TIME** 30 minutes

½ tsp (2.5 ml) sabja seeds or chia seeds
½ C (125 ml) water
4 C (1 litre) vanilla ice cream
¼ C (60 ml) rose water
¼ C (60 ml) rose syrup
4 C (1 litre) full-cream milk
1 C (250 ml) Turkish delight morsels
   (optional)
Whipped cream, for topping
   (optional)

1 Mix the sabja or chia seeds with the water In a small glass or bowl. Set aside for 20 minutes.
2 Place the ice cream, rose water, rose syrup and milk into a blender and blend until smooth.
3 Decant into large glasses and, if you like, decorate with Turkish delight morsels and whipped cream.

Sweet and Savoury Dates

Medjool dates remain my most loved because these fleshy fruits are harvested from the date palm tree and then packaged immediately. There's no processing or artificial preservation even during the packaging process. You may notice tiny specks of white powder on the dates if they've been stored, but this is perfectly normal. It's the natural sugars in the date rising to the skin. Medjool dates are perfect for smoothies and baking and one lone date is the perfect sugar balance I need with my Turkish coffee or espresso!

MAKES 24 | **PREPARATION TIME** 30 minutes

FOR THE SAVOURY DATES

24 Medjool dates, slit in the centre
    and pitted
½ C (125 ml) plain cream cheese, at
    room temperature
½ tsp (2.5 ml) freshly ground black pepper
½ Tbsp (7.5 ml) sea salt flakes
Ground, smoked paprika or cumin,
    for dusting (optional)
½ C (125 ml) pistachios, walnuts or almonds,
    roughly ground in a food processor
Honey, for drizzling (optional)

FOR THE SWEET DATES

1 C (250 ml) roasted salted almonds or
    raw almonds
24 Medjool dates, slit in the centre and pitted
250 g dark chocolate, roughly chopped
1 Tbsp (15 ml) coconut oil
½ Tbsp (7.5 ml) sea salt flakes
¼ C (60 ml) coconut flakes or desiccated
    coconut
1 tsp (5 ml) chia seeds (optional)
¼ C (60 ml) chopped nuts of choice
    (optional)

PREPARING THE SAVOURY DATES

1 Fill the centre of each date with 1 tsp (5 ml) cream cheese.
2 Top each filled date with the tiniest sprinkle of black pepper and sea salt flakes.
3 Lightly dust with ground paprika or cumin (if using).
4 Sprinkle with nut crumbles and drizzle with honey (if using) and serve.

PREPARING THE SWEET DATES

1 Insert one or two almonds, depending on size, into the open slit of each Medjool date. Set aside on a sheet of baking paper.
2 Place the dark chocolate and coconut oil into a bowl and microwave in 30 second intervals, stirring in between, until the chocolate is smooth and glossy.
3 Dip each of the almond-filled dates into the chocolate sauce until completely covered.
4 Sprinkle with desiccated coconut or coconut flakes and any of the other toppings listed, i.e. chia seeds or chopped nuts. Place on baking paper to dry.
5 Place inside the freezer for 10 minutes or the refrigerator for 20 minutes.
6 Transfer the savoury and sweet dates to a serving platter and serve right away or store inside an airtight container in the refrigerator for up to two weeks.

Cape Malay Boeber

Boeber originates from Indonesia, where it is known as burbur. The Indonesian version is much thicker than the Cape Malay boeber and is eaten as a breakfast porridge. The Cape Malay boeber is a silky sweet, warm milky drink that contains sago and vermicelli, is laced with rose water and garnished with slivers of almonds. Boeber is usually only made during Ramadan and in most Cape Malay households is served on the fifteenth night to signify the halfway mark of the fast.

SERVES 6 | **PREPARATION TIME** 15 minutes | **COOKING TIME** 45 minutes

50 g unsalted butter

2 cardamom pods, slightly bruised

3 cinnamon sticks

4 balls lokshen, crushed or 1 C (250 ml) crushed vermicelli

4 C (1 litre) full-cream milk

¼ C (60 ml) sago, soaked in tepid water for 15 minutes

½ C (125 ml) rose water

¼ tsp (1.25 ml) almond essence

½ C (125 ml) white sugar

2 Tbsp (30 ml) sliced almonds, roasted, for garnishing

2 Tbsp (30 ml) desiccated coconut, toasted, for garnishing

1 Melt the butter in a saucepan on medium heat. Add the cardamom pods and cinnamon sticks.

2 Once the spices start releasing their aromas and the butter is about to sizzle, add the crushed lokshen or vermicelli.

3 Brown slightly for about 10 minutes, stirring continuously.

4 Add the milk, sago, rose water and almond essence and simmer for at least 15–20 minutes or until the sago is translucent and the boeber has thickened.

5 Add the sugar and stir until the sugar has dissolved. Do a taste test at this stage, as additional sugar might be required depending on individual taste.

6 Adjust the heat to low and cook, covered, for a further 10 minutes.

7 Remove from the heat, ladle into individual serving bowls or glasses and garnish with slices of roasted almonds and toasted coconut before serving

CARIEMA'S TIPS

You can add sultanas in step 4. Sprinkle the cooked boeber with desiccated coconut or coconut flakes just before serving.
Bruising the cardamom slightly increases the intensity of flavour that infuses the milk.
It's important to cook all the ingredients on medium heat. Anything higher and the butter and vermicelli will be susceptible to burning.

Quick and Easy Veggie Soup

Traditionally, most Cape Malays would have split pea and vegetable soup during Ramadan, which may include soup bones or beef shin for added depth of flavour. The downside to making split pea soup is that it takes a long time to cook, which is why I turned to this recipe for a quicker option, but without sacrificing flavour.

SERVES 6–8 | **PREPARATION TIME** 20 minutes | **COOKING TIME** 50 minutes, including resting time

1 can (400 g) cannellini beans or chickpeas, rinsed and drained

3 stalks celery, including leaves, roughly chopped

1 large carrot, peeled and quartered

1 potato, peeled and quartered

1 leek, cleaned and roughly sliced

1 onion, quartered

1 Tbsp (15 ml) olive oil

1 clove garlic

1 can (400 g) Italian plum tomatoes, skinned and puréed in a food processor

Salt to taste

½ tsp (2.5 ml) freshly ground black pepper

2 Tbsp (30 ml) Ina Paarman's vegetable stock powder

6 C (1.5 litres) water

¼ C (60 ml) alphabet pasta or small macaroni pasta

Parmesan shavings, for garnishing (optional)

1. Place half the drained beans or chickpeas into a food processor and purée. Set aside in a bowl.
2. In the same food processer (no need to clean in between) and doing each of the vegetables individually, pulse three times. Set aside.
3. Heat the oil in a large saucepan on high heat and add the garlic and celery. Sauté for about 5 minutes or until fragrant.
4. Add all the prepared vegetables and give this a good mix.
5. Add the puréed tomatoes, salt, pepper, powdered stock and 4 C (1 litre) of the water. Bring to a boil, then reduce the heat to medium and simmer for 15 minutes.
6. Submerge a stick blender into the saucepan with the cooked ingredients and pulse about four times to give you a smooth but not paste-like consistency.
7. Adjust the heat to high, add half of the remaining water and bring to a boil.
8. Adjust the heat to medium, add the puréed beans, drained beans, remaining cup of water and the pasta. Cook for 15 minutes, then switch off the heat and allow to rest for 15 minutes before serving.
9. Serve in individual bowls, with shavings of Parmesan, alongside crusty bread.

Chicken Gyoza Dumplings

I can devour mounds of these little gems in no time! They are also a healthier substitute to the 'fried goodies' such as samoosas and spring rolls that we commonly have for iftar. I also find them exceptionally therapeutic to prepare and so I hardly notice how the time flies while making them. The dumplings freeze remarkably well and can be stored in a sealed container for up to three months.

MAKES 20–30 | **PREPARATION TIME** 30 minutes | **COOKING TIME** 20 minutes

FOR THE SPICY SAUCE
¼ C (60 ml) light soy sauce
2 Tbsp (30 ml) chilli sauce
1 small clove garlic, peeled and crushed
2 Tbsp (30 ml) finely sliced spring onion

FOR THE DUMPLINGS
250–300 g chicken mince
1 egg white
1 tsp (5 ml) white pepper
¼ tsp (1.25 ml) salt
½ Tbsp (7.5 ml) garlic and ginger paste
¼ C (60 ml) finely chopped fresh coriander
¼ C (60 ml) finely sliced spring onions
20–30 gyoza or wonton wrappers

PREPARING THE SAUCE
1 Mix all the sauce ingredients together in a bowl. Set aside until ready to serve.

PREPARING THE FILLING
1 Place the chicken mince, egg white, pepper, salt, garlic and ginger paste, fresh coriander and spring onions into a large bowl.
2 Mix vigorously with a fork until the mixture is 'sticky'.

SHAPING THE DUMPLINGS
1 Place a teaspoon of filling into the centre of each dumpling wrapper.
2 Moisten the edges with water and fold the wrapper over the filling. Pinch in the sides and squeeze to create two pleats.
3 Bring a large saucepan of water to a boil on high heat.
4 Add the dumplings – in batches of about 7 dumplings – and cook for about 5 minutes or until they float to the surface.
5 Use a slotted spoon to transfer the dumplings to a serving bowl. Spoon over the spicy sauce and serve warm.

Vietnamese-style Cold Spring Rolls

These spring rolls are perfect as a light summer snack, and during Ramadan they're an ideal substitute for the fried version. I also find that during Ramadan there are always leftovers from the night before so this is a great way to use up any cooked chicken, beef or prawns. I was inspired by Marion Grasby's version, where the spring rolls have edible flowers visible through the transparent rice paper sheets.

SERVES 12 | **PREPARATION TIME** 30 minutes | **COOKING TIME** 7 minutes

FOR THE SPICY PRAWNS

24 small or medium-size prawn tails, shelled and deveined

1 Tbsp (15 ml) garlic and ginger paste

1 Tbsp (15 ml) chilli sauce

2 tsp (10 ml) soy sauce

1 Tbsp (15 ml) vegetable or canola oil

FOR THE COLD SPRING ROLLS

Rice paper wrappers

Warm water in a shallow dish or tray

SUGGESTED FILLINGS:

Edible flowers • Leafy greens such as baby spinach, lettuce, Thai basil leaves, large mint leaves and so on • Rice vermicelli noodles, cooked and cooled • Chicken, cooked and shredded • Finely julienned carrot and peppers (green, yellow or orange) • Julienned cucumber

PREPARING THE SPICY PRAWNS

1 Combine the prawns, garlic and ginger paste and sauces in a mixing bowl. Set aside for 5 minutes.

2 Heat the oil in a large nonstick frying pan on high heat and add the prawns.

3 Cook for 2 minutes on each side or until cooked through and the prawns are tender and pink.

4 Transfer to a plate and set aside to cool.

ASSEMBLING THE SPRING ROLLS

1 Before you start rolling, you'll need to get all your fillings ready and cooled.

2 To assemble the cold rolls, dip a sheet of rice paper into the warm water.

3 Place the wrapper on a clean tea towel. Add your choice of fillings, then fold in the sides of the wrapper.

4 Fold the bottom of the wrapper over the filling and roll up the entire parcel into a tight, neat cylinder shape.

5 Serve the cold rolls with your favourite dipping sauce.

Peppered Steak Hand Pies

Homemade cocktail pies are a staple during Ramadan and most Cape Malay home cooks either order them from their local supplier or end up purchasing pastry and making them at home themselves. This recipe calls for pastry – both shortcrust and puff or flaky pastry – and I suggest that you go out and purchase it, instead of spending extensive hours making it at home. The filling is lush, peppery and saucy, and the meat rich and deliciously tender because it is slow-cooked for about 2 hours.

MAKES 12–14 | **PREPARATION TIME** 10 minutes | **COOKING TIME** 2 hours 30 minutes

800 g sirloin or rib-eye steak, cubed into 3 cm bite-size portions
Salt to taste
1 tsp (5 ml) freshly ground black pepper
½ C (125 ml) cake wheat flour
2 Tbsp (30 ml) canola or vegetable oil
1 large onion, finely chopped
1 clove garlic, peeled and crushed
1 C (250 ml) water
1 punnet (250 g) mushrooms, quartered (optional)
½ tsp (2.5 ml) peppercorns, roughly bruised in a pestle and mortar
2–3 sheets shortcrust pastry
2 sheets puff or flaky pastry
2 egg yolks, beaten

PREPARING THE FILLING

1 Place the steak into a bowl and season with salt and pepper. Add the flour and toss the steak portions to ensure that all the sides are coated in the flour. Set aside.

2 Heat the oil in a large saucepan on medium to high heat.

3 Tap the excess flour from the beef portions and place the cubes into the saucepan. You will need to do this in batches, as overcrowding will boil the beef instead of searing it.

4 Sear the portions on all sides for 2–3 minutes or until golden. Transfer to a plate.

5 Using the same saucepan, adjust the heat to medium and add the onion. Sauté for 3 minutes or until the onion is starting to soften. Add the garlic and cook for another minute until fragrant.

6 Add about 1 Tbsp (15 ml) of the water and use a wooden spoon or spatula to scrape up any browned bits from the bottom of the saucepan. Adjust the heat to high, add the mushrooms and peppercorns, and return the seared steak cubes to the saucepan. Give everything a good stir.

7 Add the remaining water, cover the saucepan and turn the heat down to low. Simmer gently for 2 hours, stirring every so often.

8 Once the meat is tender, transfer the filling to a bowl and let it cool completely.

ASSEMBLING THE PIES

1 Use individual pie tins or a muffin/cupcake baking tin. Spray with nonstick spray.
2 Cut the shortcrust pastry sheets into squares, slightly larger than the size of the individual muffin/cupcake moulds.
3 Line the baking tin with pastry and cut off any excess corners of pastry to fill any gaps.
4 Spoon the cooled meat filling into the shortcrust pastry cups to about three-quarters full.
5 Use a round cookie cutter or glass to cut out the puff pastry lids. (If the pastry is wrinkly or thick, roll out lightly first.)
6 Drape the pastry lid over the filling and press the sides together to seal.
7 Use a fork or your fingers to make indents in the sides of the pastry and to further seal the edges.
8 Using a sharp, pointed knife, trim off any excess pastry and poke two small slits in the top of each pie.
9 Brush the tops with the beaten egg yolks and place the pies into the refrigerator for at least 1 hour or until the pastry is cold and firm.
10 Preheat the oven to 200 °C.
11 Bake the pies in the oven for 30 minutes or until golden. Serve piping hot.

Labarang Lunch –
Cape Malay Love Language Amplified

Food is truly the love language of the Cape Malays and, on Eid day, it's spoken in subtle tones of saffron, in the form of a regal biryani (page 101). You'll feel the warmth of family and feasting when you pull up a chair and gently lay your napkin on your lap, readying yourself for slivers of slow-cooked leg of lamb (page 96) nestled on top of honey-sweet yellow rice with morsels of the golden, glistening sultanas. Our love language comes alive as whispers of spices delicately flavour our traditional crayfish curry (page 110) or prawn curry, to enhance the sweetness of the shellfish.

Our Eid lunch brings with it abundance and extravagance, but none of this is for ourselves, it's all to share and indulge in with friends, family and guests. The beauty of our love language is more prominent on this day, as we give thanks for the feast before us, but also reminisce about the many Eid lunches in the homes of our parents, grandparents and family. It's for this reason that I couldn't think of any other foodie and home cook but the talented Monowara (Nouri) Mohamed Bhamjee, who I met at a foodie event in Port Elizabeth, in the Eastern Cape in South Africa.

Nouri, as we know her, was born in Paarl in the Western Cape, but moved to Gqeberha, formerly Port Elizabeth, in the Eastern Cape with her family when she was only eight years old. Though her father cooked and catered for weddings, it was her mom, Zainunisa Antar Mohamed, who was an ardent baker and influenced Nouri's dexterity for baking at a young age. Her skill can be seen in thousands of images posted on her Facebook page – an array of airy sponge cakes, covered in fresh cream and drizzled with chocolate sauce. Her desserts will have you abandoning any calorie count and her doughnuts, whether plain or dunked into a caramel glaze and topped with crushed hazelnuts, will satisfy any of your sweet-tooth cravings!

Nouri always smiles warmly when she reminisces about growing up on Cape Malay dishes, bredies and curries, and the fusion for her is in the Indian flavour twist! She is the quintessential domestic goddess, catering for events, cooking and baking for her family and friends and creating scrumptious menus and meals. It's therefore fitting that Nouri's 'presence' finds itself in the words, paragraphs and recipes that reside in this part of my 'Together as One' chapter. She invites everyone to her table, to grab a seat, a plate, a comfortable place where the only language spoken is love ... especially on Eid day!

Labarang Biscuit Bounty

No Eid table is complete without an ornately adorned Eid cake, which serves as the alluring centrepiece, and a flamboyant display of Eid biscuits. This tradition is no different to the Eid traditions in Indonesia and Malaysia, where biscuits and sweet meats adorn beautifully laid Eid tables. The size of the biscuits is smaller in comparison to our traditional Cape Malay ones, which makes it even more delightful when displayed. They're the ideal accompaniment to the mandatory cup of tea any guest would be offered as you are welcomed into our homes on Eid day.

I wanted to pause a little while putting this chapter together. It holds so much meaning for me because my mom always seemed to create the perfect setting for our home during Eid and our Eid table was no exception. To this day, it's impossible for me to ignore how overcome I am with emotion, as I have such vivid memories of laying our Eid table with my mom. Since the fondest recollections are of our Eid cake and dessert table, I wanted to bare my soul through the images you'll see on the pages that follow. This was my mother's display of love on Eid day, and I am forever grateful to be able to bring it to life through this chapter.

Malaysian Butter Biscuits
with a White Chocolate and Pistachio Topping

These biscuits are unique in that they contain rolled oats. It's a recipe that Rita Zahara's mom customised for Eid and it's featured in Rita's cookbook *Malay Heritage Cooking*. She vows that this has become a staple at Eid in their home and, suffice to say, it's found its rightful place on my Eid table too.

MAKES 90 | **PREPARATION TIME** 30 minutes | **BAKING TIME** 12 minutes

200 g unsalted butter, at room temperature

½ C (125 ml) castor sugar

2 tsp (10 ml) vanilla essence

¼ C (60 ml) rolled oats, roughly chopped in a food processor

Pinch of salt

¾ C (200 ml) self-raising wheat flour , sifted

1¼ C (310 ml) cake wheat flour , sifted

½ tsp (2.5 ml) baking powder

150 g white chocolate, chopped and melted

1 C (250 ml) pistachio slivers, lightly roasted in the oven or on the stovetop

Gold leaf or gold dust (optional)

1. Preheat the oven to 160 ºC.
2. Line at least two baking trays with baking paper and set aside.
3. In the bowl of an electric mixer, fitted with the paddle attachment, cream the butter and castor sugar until light and fluffy.
4. Add the vanilla essence, rolled oats, salt, flours and baking powder and mix to form a unified biscuit dough.
5. The dough is very soft and can be shaped using a cookie press gun. Alternatively, roll it out on a lightly floured surface to a thickness of 3–4 mm and use a cookie cutter to shape the biscuits.
6. Arrange the biscuits on the baking trays.
7. Bake for approximately 12 minutes or until the biscuits are golden. The biscuits will be soft while hot, but will harden as they cool.
8. Set aside on a wire rack until cool.
9. Dip the biscuits into the melted chocolate and scatter with pistachio chips. Set aside until the chocolate has set.
10. To create that Eid glitz and glamour, adorn with bits of gold leaf or sprinkle with gold dust.

Malaysian-inspired Prosperity Biscuits
(Kuih Makmur)

The late Faldela Williams, author of *The Cape Malay Cookbook*, has a biscuit recipe that resembles this traditional Malay prosperity biscuit. Her version is what we as Cape Malays know as Angel Whispers, closely resembling another Cape Malay favourite named Melting Moments. One of the reasons I love this recipe is that the appearance of the biscuit is unassuming, but the cashew filling on the inside is what will make you ask for seconds and thirds.

MAKES 50 | **PREPARATION TIME** 30 minutes | **BAKING TIME** 12 minutes

FOR THE FILLING
20 g salted butter
½ C (125 ml) cashew nuts, pecan nuts
   or walnuts, finely chopped
1 tsp (5 ml) castor sugar

FOR THE BISCUITS
125 g unsalted butter, at room temperature
1 C (250 ml) icing sugar
1 large egg, beaten
2 Tbsp (30 ml) evaporated milk
1 tsp (5 ml) vanilla essence
Pinch of salt
1 C (250 ml) self-raising wheat flour , sifted
1 C (250 ml) cake wheat flour , sifted
¼ C (60 ml) cornflour
Icing sugar, for dusting

PREPARING THE FILLING
1. Melt the butter in a saucepan on medium heat.
2. Add the nuts and castor sugar, and combine to form a crumbly filling. Set aside.

PREPARING THE BISCUITS
1. Preheat the oven to 180 °C.
2. Line two baking trays with baking paper and set aside.
3. In the bowl of an electric mixer, fitted with the paddle attachment, cream the butter and icing sugar until light and fluffy.
4. Add the beaten egg, evaporated milk, vanilla essence, salt and flours, and mix to form a unified biscuit dough.
5. Roll out on a lightly floured surface to 3–4 mm thick.
6. Use a round cookie cutter to shape the biscuits. Place a cut-out circle in the palm of your hand and then add ½ tsp (2.5 ml) of the filling. Bring the edges together and shape the dough with your hands to form a ball.
7. Place on the floured surface and shape it into a round cookie shape, and then arrange on the baking trays.
8. Bake for about 12 minutes or until slightly golden.
9. Set aside on a wire rack until cool. Dust with icing sugar.

Cadbury Flake Biscuits

This biscuit was very popular in the 1990s and resembles a Cadbury flake chocolate – it is chocolate indulgence on another level! My guidance to you would be to ensure that you use Cadbury chocolate both for the coating and for the dough – any other substitute, such as cooking chocolate, will detract from the richness and that distinctive Cadbury flavour.

MAKES 30 | **PREPARATION TIME** 30 minutes | **BAKING TIME** 10 minutes

FOR THE TOPPING

1 large slab (230 g) Cadbury's plain milk
   chocolate, roughly chopped
1 bag (204 g) mini Cadbury Flake
   chocolates or 10 mini flakes

FOR THE BISCUITS

250 g unsalted butter, at room temperature
1 C (250 ml) icing sugar, sifted
1 egg
1 Tbsp (15 ml) vanilla essence
Pinch of salt
2½ C (625 ml) cake wheat flour , sifted
¼ C (60 ml) cornflour
1 tsp (5 ml) cream of tartar
½ C (125 ml) cocoa powder, sifted
2 large Cadbury Flake chocolates, crushed

PREPARING THE TOPPING

1   Place the roughly chopped chocolate into a bowl and microwave in 30-second bursts until the chocolate has melted. Set aside.

PREPARING THE BISBUITS

1   Preheat the oven to 180 °C.
2   Line a baking tray with baking paper and set aside.
3   In the bowl of an electric mixer, fitted with the paddle attachment, cream the butter and icing sugar until light and fluffy.
4   Add the egg and mix again until light and fluffy.
5   Add the vanilla essence, salt, flours, cream of tartar, cocoa powder and crushed chocolate crumbles and mix to form a unified biscuit dough.
6   Place the dough on a lightly floured surface and roll it out into a square or rectangular shape that is about 1 cm thick.
7   Use a fork to create the lines on the biscuit to resemble the chocolate flake.
8   Use a knife and a ruler to cut the biscuits into portions of 1.5–2 cm wide and 6 cm long. Transfer the shaped biscuits to the lined baking tray and bake for 10 minutes.
9   Transfer to a wire rack to cool for about 5 minutes, then drizzle the melted chocolate over the biscuits.
10 Crumble the flake chocolates over the melted chocolate or cut them into portions and place on top.
11 The biscuits can be stored for up to three months in an airtight container.

Cape Malay Soetkoekies

This aromatic biscuit is a perfect representation of the Dutch influence in some of our Cape Malay dishes, as it closely resembles the flavours one would find in the traditional, spiced Dutch cookie called 'speculaas'. Our Cape Malay version mostly makes its appearance during Eid celebrations. In Cape Town and most parts of South Africa this biscuit is known as a 'soetkoekie'. It is infused with ground ginger, cinnamon, cloves and nutmeg. The biscuit is two-toned – one side is dull and beige while the other is stained a deep crimson colour, which is derived from the red bolus. Cape Malays still refer to this food colouring as 'rooi bol'. The biscuit dough is cut into a heart or flower shape and adorned with a peanut half. I've been told that the very best of its kind is made in Port Elizabeth, where it is referred to as an 'essie' because the dough is rolled into thinnish cylinders and moulded into an S-shape.

MAKES 30 | **PREPARATION TIME** 10 minutes | **BAKING TIME** 10 minutes

500 g cake wheat flour

1 C (250 ml) ground almonds

1 tsp (5 ml) bicarbonate of soda

2 C (500 ml) brown or yellow sugar

1 tsp (5 ml) ground nutmeg

1 tsp (5 ml) ground cloves

1 tsp (5 ml) ground cinnamon or
    mixed spice

1 tsp (5 ml) ground ginger

250 g unsalted butter, at room
    temperature

100 ml canola or sunflower oil

1 egg, lightly whisked or beaten

1 tsp (5 ml) red bolus (rooi bol)

Peanut halves, for decorating

1. Preheat the oven to 200 ºC.
2. Line a baking tray with baking paper and set aside.
3. Sift the flour, ground almonds, bicarbonate of soda and ground spices together in a mixing bowl. Set aside.
4. In the bowl of an electric mixer, fitted with the paddle attachment, cream the butter until light and fluffy.
5. Add the oil and beaten egg and mix well.
6. Gradually add the sifted dry ingredients to form a stiff but pliable dough.
7. Take a third of the dough and mix in the red colouring until it has changed to a uniform colour. Set aside.
8. Roll out the remaining dough on a lightly floured surface to a thickness of 5 mm.
9. Place little bits or balls of the dyed dough on top of the rolled-out dough and roll out again to a thickness of 5 mm.
10. Use a cookie cutter to cut into shapes and place a peanut half on the cut-out shape.
11. Transfer the biscuits onto the lined baking tray.
12. Bake for 10 minutes, then transfer to a wire rack to cool.

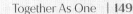

Shamila Mollajee's Chocolate Éclairs and Profiteroles

This recipe developed from a virtual masterclass given to me by my friend Shamila. I still have the video where she walks me through the perfect way to make chocolate éclairs and while I would like to take credit for some of the small tweaks I have made, it's truly her guidance that created these perfect little éclairs and baby profiteroles!

MAKES 15–20 | **PREPARATION TIME** 30 minutes | **BAKING TIME** 25 minutes

FOR THE CHANTILLY CREAM

2 C (500 ml) cold whipping cream or
    double cream
½ Tbsp (7.5 ml) icing sugar, sifted
½ tsp (2.5 ml) vanilla essence

FOR THE CHOCOLATE GANACHE

1 slab (100 g) Lindt dark chocolate
1 large slab (230 g) Cadbury's plain
    milk chocolate
¼ C (60 ml) single cream, warmed in
    the microwave
1 Tbsp (15 ml) honey

FOR THE ÉCLAIRS

100 g unsalted butter, at room
    temperature
Pinch of salt
1 C (250 ml) water
1 C (250 ml) cake wheat flour , sifted
3 eggs, at room temperature
1 egg, beaten

PREPARING THE CHANTILLY CREAM

1. Place all the ingredients into a mixing bowl and whisk until the cream has formed stiff peaks.
2. Cover with plastic wrap and set aside in the refrigerator until needed.

PREPARING THE CHOCOLATE GANACHE

1. Place the dark and milk chocolates into a bowl and microwave in 30-second bursts until the chocolate has melted.
2. Add the cream and honey and mix to form a smooth and glossy ganache.

PREPARING THE ÉCLAIRS

1. Preheat the oven to 200 ºC.
2. Line a baking tray with baking paper and set aside.
3. Place the butter, salt and water into a medium-size saucepan on medium to high heat, and bring to a boil.
4. Adjust the heat to low and add all the flour, mixing vigorously with a wooden spoon until the mixture resembles a big ball of dough. Remove from the heat and set aside for 10 minutes.

5 Transfer the dough to the bowl of an electric mixer, fitted with the paddle attachment, and set the speed to medium.

6 Add the first three eggs, one at a time, ensuring that you mix well between additions.

7 At this stage, check the consistency of the dough. If it is stiff, add the whole beaten egg. If it is flexible but not mushy, add only half the beaten egg.

8 Use a piping bag to shape the éclairs or a spoon to drop spoonsful onto the baking tray for the profiteroles.

9 Bake at 200 ºC for 10 minutes, then adjust the oven temperature to 170 ºC and bake for another 7–10 minutes until well risen, crisp and golden.

SHAMILA'S TIPS

After the éclairs or profiteroles have baked, slit them in half and then bake them for a further 3–5 minutes to dry out the moisture. This creates a crispier outer shell that will be able to hold the cream and chocolate sauce well.

Once baked, transfer to a cooling rack and cool completely.

Fill with the Chantilly cream and coat with chocolate ganache. Decorate as desired.

CARIEMA'S TIPS

Profiteroles: Pipe walnut-size rounds (for small buns) or golf-ball size rounds (for big buns) of the mixture onto the baking tray, spacing them well apart. They will rise and expand to close to double their original size.

Avoid pointed tops: Before baking, dip a finger into water and tap it onto any unruly peaks on the piped éclairs or profiteroles to settle them.

If you notice that the baked pastry is a bit eggy, return the profiteroles or éclairs to the oven for a few minutes and keep an eye on them.

Pecan Nut Tart
with a Chocolate-coconut Biscuit Crust

This started out as a 'Romany Cream'-style biscuit but seeing that it is so popular in our home, I began playing around with variations. I realised that I could turn the original biscuit dough into a crust and all I needed was a delectable filling. Et voilà, one of our favourite Eid desserts was born!

SERVES 8 | **PREPARATION TIME** 20 minutes | **BAKING TIME** 15 minutes

FOR THE BISCUIT CRUST

1 C (250 ml) desiccated coconut

1½ C (375 ml) cake wheat flour

1 C (250 ml) cocoa powder

½ tsp (2.5 ml) baking powder

¼ tsp (1.25 ml) salt

175 g unsalted butter, at room temperature

½ C (125 ml) castor sugar or soft brown sugar

1 egg

1 tsp (5 ml) vanilla essence

FOR THE CHOCOLATE GANACHE AND PECAN FILLING

1½ C (375 ml) semi-sweet Hershey's chocolate chips or a mixture of dark and milk chocolate

1 C (250 ml) heavy or double cream

1 C (250 ml) pecan nuts, roughly chopped (reserve some for decorating)

PREPARING THE BISCUIT CRUST

1. Set the oven on the grill setting, on high.
2. Spread out the coconut on a baking tray and toast it for about 30 seconds or until the white coconut flakes turn golden. Give the baking tray a shake and toast for another 30 seconds. Keep your eye on this because it can darken quite quickly depending on how hot the oven is.
3. Sift the flour, cocoa powder, baking powder and salt into a mixing bowl and set aside.
4. Remove the coconut from the oven and set aside in a bowl.
5. Adjust the oven to your normal baking setting and preheat to 180 °C.
6. Place the butter and castor sugar into the bowl of an electric mixer, fitted with the paddle attachment, and cream together until pale and fluffy.
7. Add the egg and continue mixing until all the ingredients are well incorporated.
8. Keep the mixer setting on a medium speed and add the vanilla essence.
9. Add the sifted dry ingredients into the bowl and mix on a low speed until all the ingredients gradually come together to form a soft dough.
10. Remove the bowl from the mixer. Add the toasted coconut to the dough (reserve 1–2 Tbsp [15–30 ml] for decorating). Use a spatula or wooden spoon to mix this together.

11 I've used a rectangular nonstick tart tin measuring 36 × 13 cm. Grease the tin with nonstick spray and then line the tin with the dough.

12 To line the tin, simply take a few pieces of dough and mould them in the tin with your fingers, until the dough is spread out evenly and is 3–4 mm thick. You may have excess dough left (depending on the size of the baking tin you use), which you can use for a batch of cookies or biscuits. Alternatively, you can store it in the freezer for up to three months.

13 Line the dough with baking paper and baking beans (or just normal dehydrated beans) and blind bake for 12–15 minutes. The tart shell may feel a bit spongy, but it will harden as it cools down. Set aside on a wire rack.

PREPARING THE FILLING

1 Place the chocolate chips in a bowl and set aside.

2 Heat the heavy or double cream in a saucepan on medium to high heat. Once the cream starts simmering for about 30 seconds, remove it from the heat.

3 Pour the warm cream over the chocolate and mix well until it forms a smooth chocolate ganache.

4 Add the chopped pecan nuts and pour the filling into the cooled tart shell.

5 Decorate the tart with the reserved chopped pecan nuts and toasted coconut.

6 Refrigerate for about 2 hours.

7 Serve with clotted or lightly whipped cream.

Labarang Konfyt

I am sure there are so many shortcuts to make watermelon konfyt (preserve), but because this sweet treat was taught to me by Aunty Bhebi, my friend Shamila Mollajee's mother, I simply do not want to alter the original recipe. Be prepared for overnight soaking and a 7-hour cooking process – the result is nothing short of sweet and sticky indulgence!

MAKES ABOUT 4 × 352 g jars | **PREPARATION TIME** 20 minutes | **COOKING TIME** 7 hours

FOR THE SLAKED LIME SOLUTION
10 C (2.5 litres) water
1 Tbsp (15 ml) slaked lime powder
½ tsp (2.5 ml) bicarbonate of soda

FOR THE KONFYT
1 kg of the inner white flesh of the
   watermelon, skin and ripe flesh removed
1 kg white or brown sugar
8 C (2 litres) water, plus extra for topping up
1 Tbsp (15 ml) lemon juice
1 thumb-size piece fresh ginger, peeled
   and sliced
1 Tbsp (15 ml) ground ginger

PREPARING THE SLAKED LIME SOLUTION
1 Pour the water into a large container with a lid. Add the lime and bicarbonate of soda and mix well. Set aside.

PREPARING THE KONFYT
1 Cut the white flesh of the watermelon into portions of 5–6 cm in length and 4–5 cm wide.
2 Use a fork to poke holes into the watermelon portions, back and front and on the sides.
3 Submerge all the watermelon portions in the slaked lime solution, making sure that the water covers the watermelon. Seal the container and leave overnight.
4 The following day, drain the soaked watermelon portions in a large colander and rinse under running water for about 1 minute.
5 Transfer the watermelon portions to a large saucepan on high heat. Add the remaining konfyt ingredients and bring to a boil.
6 After every 30–40 minutes, check the water level. Keep on topping up with water until the watermelon is tender and the liquid has reduced to a syrup.
7 Cut into bite-size pieces and serve on a small plate with a cake fork.

CARIEMA'S TIPS

If you can't get your hands on slaked lime powder, then omit it, but increase the bicarbonate of soda to 3 Tbsp (45 ml). It will not compromise the taste.

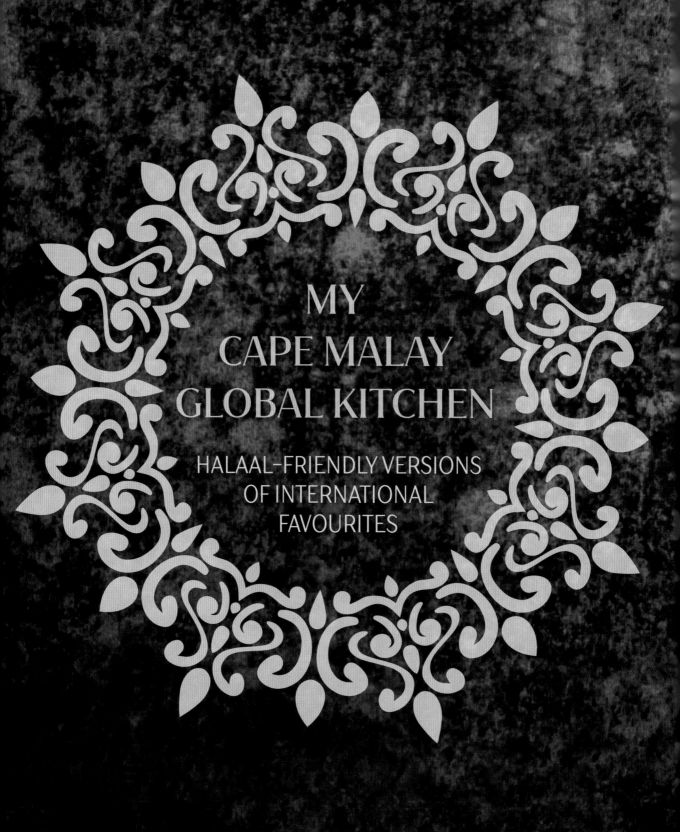

MY
CAPE MALAY
GLOBAL KITCHEN

HALAAL-FRIENDLY VERSIONS
OF INTERNATIONAL
FAVOURITES

There are a few elements that have largely influenced my experimentation and love for food beyond my South African culinary roots, namely: living and working abroad, my travels to other countries, studying to become a chef and the ever-changing palates of my two sons. They have spurred on new culinary creations in my home kitchen and adaptations of some of the more traditional Cape Malay fare. The skills and knowledge I acquired at culinary school made it so much easier for me to create an authentic Italian risotto, for instance, before I started to customise it.

I also go through 'foodie phases', when I will crave an Asian stir-fry or dumplings and then frequent a local restaurant or café. Eventually, I will venture to YouTube and experiment with recipes and customise them to my and my family's liking. As I learn and fail, and succeed, my confidence is finally borne out by my insatiable need to get the recipe 'just right'. The recipes in this chapter are testimony to how much my own Cape Malay palate has evolved. It also demonstrates that transforming our much-loved restaurant and café meals into Halaal-friendly ones does not compromise flavour.

In this chapter, global dishes that would traditionally contain pork or alcohol have been customised to suit Halaal dietary requirements. Flavour is derived from a mix of spices and seasonings. I turn up the volume with a combination of store-bought sauces – especially for the Asian recipes – and all of these are Halaal-based. You'll also notice that many of the dishes contain garlic and ginger, chilli flakes, fresh chillies or cayenne pepper – again appealing to my Cape Malay culinary roots, where heat is essential!

My inspiration for this chapter comes from Fayruza Abrahams, who resides in Bo-Kaap, the Cape Malay Quarter. She maintains that food is not a thing, but rather a feeling, and she introduces spicy, scrumptious and distinctive flavours of Cape Malay cuisine via her cooking classes. Fayruza is no stranger to the public. Apart from her cooking classes and her food blog *tastemalay*, she was also a judge with Zola Nene and Fritz Schoon on *Taste Master South Africa*. It was therefore no surprise when she was invited by Chef Alisa Reynolds, the owner of Los Angeles restaurant My 2 Cents, to be a contributor on the Hulu Disney-produced food show called *In Search of Soul Food*.

Fayruza is also well travelled, from London to New York, Paris to China and a whole lot of cities in between, she's sampled food across continents. It's therefore almost second nature to her to come home and customise the dishes she's tasted through her travels. When asked which cuisine she loves most, her answer is 'Asian – food from Thailand, China, Singapore!' – and that just happens to be another reason why she and I get on like a house on fire!

Easy Asian Stir-fry

I love stir-fry dishes because they are versatile and making my own means that I get to serve it immediately, right from the wok to the bowl. This recipe is inspired by Simply Asia in Cape Town and it has become a staple in our home when it comes to stir-fries. Though the restaurant serves a beef, chicken or prawn version, I love doing a combo – a bit of each, packed with flavour!

SERVES 4 | **PREPARATION TIME** 15 minutes | **COOKING TIME** 20 minutes

2 packets (70 g each) 2-minute noodles

4 C (1 litre) boiling water

1 Tbsp (15 ml) sesame oil or any standard cooking oil

250–300 g steak, cut into 12–15 strips

4–6 dried red chillies or ½ Tbsp (7.5 ml) roasted chilli paste or a combination of both

1 large chicken breast fillet, cut into 12–15 strips

10 shrimps or prawn tails, deveined and peeled

1 Tbsp (15 ml) garlic and ginger paste

1 Tbsp (15 ml) dark soy sauce

1 Tbsp (15 ml) light soy or traditional soy sauce

1 Tbsp (15 ml) oyster sauce or stir-fry sauce of choice

375 g stir-fry vegetables of choice

Handful of raw cashew nuts (optional)

1 thumb-size piece fresh ginger, peeled and julienned

1 sprig fresh coriander

1. Place the 2-minute noodles (noodles only, you may discard the sachets of sauce and seasoning) in a bowl, add the boiling water, cover with plastic wrap and set aside.
2. Heat the oil in a large wok or frying pan on high heat.
3. When the oil is hot, add the beef strips and stir-fry for 2 minutes.
4. Add the red chillies or chilli paste, the chicken strips and shrimps or prawns, along with the garlic and ginger paste and stir-fry for 5 minutes.
5. Add the sauces and vegetables (along with the cashew nuts, if using) and stir-fry for about 3 minutes.
6. Drain the noodles and add them to the stir-fry. Give everything a good mix.
7. Remove from the heat, garnish with julienned slices of ginger and fresh coriander. Serve hot.

Mongolian Beef

Despite its name, the dish has nothing to do with Mongolian cuisine. It is an Asian stir-fry that consists of sliced beef (typically flank steak), generally paired with lots of spring onions. It's not spicy, but does have that distinctive sweet, caramelised flavour that goes so well with sticky white or brown rice. Grab a bowl and chopsticks, and pull up a chair – you're going to come back for seconds!

SERVES 6 | **PREPARATION TIME** 20 minutes | **COOKING TIME** 10 minutes

FOR THE SAUCE

1 Tbsp (15 ml) soy sauce
½ C (125 ml) dark brown sugar
3 cloves garlic, peeled and crushed
1 thumb-size piece fresh ginger, peeled and grated
2 tsp (10 ml) canola or sunflower oil
½ C (125 ml) water

FOR THE MONGOLIAN BEEF

500 g rump or fillet steak, thinly sliced and cut into 4 × 3 cm portions
¼ C (60 ml) cornflour
1 tsp (5 ml) meat tenderiser
½ C (125 ml) canola or sunflower oil
2 spring onions, the white stalks thinly sliced and the green stalks cut into 4 cm lengths

PREPARING THE SAUCE

1   Place all the sauce ingredients into a medium-size saucepan on high heat and whisk together until the sugar has dissolved.
2   Bring the sauce to a boil, then reduce the heat to medium and simmer for about 10 minutes or until the sauce has thickened slightly. Remove from the heat and set aside.

PREPARING THE MONGOLIAN BEEF

1   Line a large plate or platter with two layers of paper towel. Set aside.
2   Place the steak strips into a large bowl, then coat with the cornflour and meat tenderiser.
3   Heat the oil in a large frying pan or wok on medium to high heat. Add the beef and fry for 1–2 minutes on each side, until golden and cooked through.
4   Transfer to the paper towel-lined plate to drain the excess oil.
5   Using the same pan or wok, adjust the heat to medium. Return the beef to the pan or wok and stir in the cooked sauce.
6   Simmer gently for 2–3 minutes until the sauce thickens further. Stir in the spring onions.
7   Serve immediately, alongside sticky white jasmine or brown rice.

Kung Pao Chicken
with Bean Sprouts

What I love most about this dish is that it contains no starch and helps to keep one's calorie count at bay. The mound of bean sprouts gives this stir-fry a pleasant and fresh crunch. You can forego the peanuts and garnish with sesame seeds instead.

SERVES 6 | **PREPARATION TIME** 15 minutes | **COOKING TIME** 20 minutes

½ C (125 ml) raw peanuts

2 Tbsp (30 ml) canola or sunflower oil

500 g skinless chicken breast fillets, cut into bite-size pieces

½ tsp (2.5 ml) salt

½ tsp (2.5 ml) freshly ground black pepper

1 Tbsp (15 ml) garlic and ginger paste

1 C (250 ml) bite-size cubes red pepper

1 C (250 ml) bite-size cubes yellow or orange pepper

1 C (250 ml) thinly sliced celery

4–6 fresh or dried red chillies (optional)

¾ C (200 ml) store-bought Kung Pao sauce

2 spring onions, thinly sliced

300 g mung bean sprouts, warmed in the microwave just before serving

1. Roast the peanuts in a small pan on medium to high heat until fragrant, then set aside.
2. Heat 1 Tbsp (15 ml) of the oil in a large wok or frying pan on medium to high heat.
3. Add the chicken to the wok or pan and season with salt and pepper. Stir-fry for 6–8 minutes or until the chicken portions are cooked.
4. Add 1 tsp (5 ml) of the garlic and ginger paste and stir-fry for another 30 seconds. Transfer to a bowl and set aside.
5. Using the same wok or pan, add the remaining oil and garlic and ginger paste. Add the peppers and celery and stir-fry for about 3 minutes until lightly browned.
6. Return the cooked chicken to the wok or pan (reserve the juices in the bowl). Add the whole chillies (if using) and stir-fry for about 1 minute.
7. Add the Kung Pao sauce and peanuts and cook about 1 minute or until the sauce has thickened.
8. Remove from the heat, stir in the spring onions and serve on top of a layer of warmed beans sprouts.

CARIEMA'S TIPS

In a small bowl, add 1 tablespoon (15 ml) balsamic vinegar, 1.5 tablespoons (22.5ml) hoisin sauce and 2 tablespoons (30 ml) soy sauce. Add this sauce in step 7, along with the rest of the ingredients in this step. This creates further depth to the deep and rich Asian flavour.

Movie-night Nachos

Saturday night is movie night at home, where we kick off our shoes and gather as a family to relax and watch a movie. This very popular Mexican dish has become our staple movie-night snack. Ensure that you use plain (not flavoured) Mexican tortilla chips, since this won't detract from the flavours of the chilli con carne or the cheese. I've also added a quick and easy way to make homemade guacamole, which is (in our home) an essential accompaniment to our nachos.

SERVES 6 | **PREPARATION TIME** 30 minutes | **COOKING TIME** 30 minutes

FOR THE GUACAMOLE

Salt to taste

1 clove garlic, peeled and crushed

¼ C (60 ml) finely chopped red onion

Juice of 1 large or 2 medium-size lemons

3–4 ripe avocados, halved and pips removed

1 tsp (5 ml) freshly ground black pepper

3 dashes hot sauce or Tabasco sauce

3 sprigs fresh coriander, stalks finely chopped and leaves roughly chopped

PREPARING THE GUACAMOLE

1   Using a pestle and mortar, gently pound the salt, garlic and onion together to form a fairly smooth paste, but with some bits and chunks in place.

2   Squeeze over the lemon juice and mix well. (The lemon juice helps to eliminate the sharpness of the raw onion.) .

3   Scoop out the flesh of the avocados into a bowl. Add the pepper, hot sauce and the onion and garlic mixture.

4   Using a fork, break down the avocado and combine with all the ingredients. At this stage, you can decide whether you want a chunky texture, which means light mixing is required. If you prefer a smoother texture, then mix the ingredients together vigorously.

5   Add the fresh coriander and stir into the avocado mixture. Do a taste test and adjust the seasoning if required. Squeeze the juice of a quarter lemon on top. Cover with plastic wrap and set aside in the refrigerator.

(Continued overleaf)

CARIEMA'S TIP

To tame the pungency of the red onion, sprinkle the chopped onions with a good pinch of coarse salt or sea salt flakes and massage with your fingers for about a minute. Rinse and drain, and squeeze out the excess water.

FOR THE CHILLI CON CARNE

2 Tbsp (30 ml) olive oil

1 large onion, finely chopped

2 cloves garlic, peeled and minced

700 g beef mince

Salt to taste

½ tsp (2.5 ml) freshly ground black pepper

1 Tbsp (15 ml) tomato paste

1 can (400 g) whole Italian tomatoes,
  skinned and puréed

1 tsp (5 ml) smoked paprika

1 tsp (5 ml) ground cumin

1 tsp (5 ml) cayenne pepper, or less
  for a milder version (optional)

1 tsp (5 ml) dried oregano

1 Tbsp (15 ml) white sugar

½ can (200 g) red kidney beans, rinsed
  and drained

2 Tbsp (30 ml) finely chopped fresh
  flat-leaf parsley, for garnishing

FOR THE NACHOS

2 bags (250 g each) plain tortilla or
  multigrain chips

1 C (250 ml) grated yellow Cheddar cheese
  and 1 C (250 ml) grated white Cheddar
  cheese, mixed together in a bowl

1 C (250 ml) sour cream

PREPARING THE CHILLI CON CARNE

1 Heat the oil in a large saucepan on medium to high heat.
  Add the onion and sauté for 5–6 minutes until lightly
  golden. Add the garlic and fry for another minute.

2 Add the beef mince, salt and pepper and cook for
  8–10 minutes or until the beef is completed cooked and
  the moisture has evaporated. Stir frequently to break
  down the mince into a crumbly texture.

3 Add the tomato paste and purée and bring to a steady
  simmer or bubble on medium heat.

4 Add the spices, oregano and sugar and simmer for
  5 minutes, stirring frequently.

5 Adjust the heat to low and then add the beans, Simmer
  for about 5 minutes.

6 Garnish with the chopped parsley and set aside.

ASSEMBLING THE NACHOS

1 Preheat the oven on the grill setting at 220 °C.

2 Line a baking tray or a large overproof dish with baking
  paper and spread out the tortilla chips in an even layer.
  Try to cover the surface so that you have no gaps showing.
  Don't worry if the chips overlap, this is perfectly fine.

3 Spoon generous amounts of the chilli con carne all
  over the chips, ensuring that each chip has a bit of chilli
  con carne on it.

4 Sprinkle with the grated cheese and grill in the oven for
  4–5 minutes or until the cheese has melted and the chilli
  con carne is heated through.

5 Serve with a dollop of guacamole and sour cream.

Mushroom Risotto
with a Truffle Oil Drizzle

If you've ever seen the movie *Eat, Pray, Love* you'll remember the scene where Liz, played by Julia Roberts, sits in a restaurant courtyard in Italy indulging in a plate of spaghetti. The entire scene spoke volumes about how something so simple could be so invigorating. It reverberates with the fullness we feel when we indulge in simple pleasures and the simplicity of finding those moments when we stop to enjoy life. This risotto is that for me – the art of eating something so simple and the enjoyment of the moment.

4 C (1 litre) vegetable stock or 3 Tbsp
   (45 ml) vegetable stock powder
   mixed with 4 C (1 litre) water
2 Tbsp (30 ml) olive oil, divided
50 g butter
400 g mixed mushrooms
1 tsp (5 ml) freshly ground black pepper
1 onion, finely chopped
1 clove garlic, peeled and crushed
2 C (500 ml) Arborio rice
Salt to taste
½ C (125 ml) fresh cream (increase to 1 C
   [250 ml] for a creamier consistency)
1 C (250 ml) grated Parmesan cheese
Chopped fresh flat-leaf parsley,
   for garnishing
Truffle oil, for drizzling

1 Warm the stock or water mixture in a small saucepan on a medium heat. Keep this simmering very gently throughout the cooking process.

2 Heat 1 Tbsp (15 ml) of the oil and half of the butter in a medium-size saucepan on medium to high heat.

3 Add the mushrooms and pepper and sauté for 7 minutes, stirring occasionally, until the mushrooms have shrunk considerably and have taken on a deep, golden brown colour. Remove the mushrooms from the pan and set aside. Reserve ¼ C (60 ml) of the mushrooms for garnishing.

4 Using the same saucepan, melt the remaining butter and oil on medium to high heat.

5 Add the onion and adjust the heat to medium. Sauté for 5 minutes or until the onion is softened and translucent.

6 Add the garlic and cook for about 1 minute until fragrant.

7 Add the rice and salt and cook for 5 minutes, stirring continuously, until the rice looks translucent and gives off a faint nutty aroma.

8 While stirring continuously, pour a ladleful of the warm stock over the rice and cook until the liquid has evaporated completely, which may take between 3 and 5 minutes.

9 Repeat this process until all the stock has been used and the rice is al dente, not mushy.

10 Turn down the heat to low and return the mushrooms to the saucepan. Add the cream and Parmesan and fold all the ingredients together. Cover the saucepan with a lid and let the risotto rest for about 3 minutes on low heat.

11 When you're ready to serve, scoop ladlesful of the risotto into a serving dish or individual bowls, garnish with the reserved mushrooms and chopped parsley, and drizzle with truffle oil.

CARIEMA'S TIP

For a smoother, velvety risotto add a generous dollop of butter towards the end, then gently fold together into the warm risotto.

Spaghetti Bolognaise

For this recipe I prefer to fold the cooked spaghetti into the sauce at the end. This adds flavour to the spaghetti that on its own can be quite bland. Since Cape Malays love spicy food, you'll often find us adding chilli flakes just before serving or a green chilli oil condiment to give a hit of heat, bite after bite.

SERVES 4–6 | **PREPARATION TIME** 10 minutes | **COOKING TIME** 40 minutes

2 Tbsp (30 ml) olive oil

1 onion, finely chopped

1 clove garlic, crushed

Salt to taste

700 g beef or lamb mince

1 can (400 g) whole Italian tomatoes, skinned and roughly puréed

¼ C (60 ml) tomato paste

3 Tbsp (45 ml) white sugar

½ Tbsp (7.5 ml) freshly ground black pepper

1 tsp (5 ml) dried Italian herbs or 1–2 sprigs fresh thyme

½ packet (250 g) spaghetti, cooked as per package instructions

½ C (125 ml) grated Parmesan cheese

Green chilli oil (page 191), for serving

1 Heat the oil in a large saucepan on medium to high heat.

2 Add the onion and sauté for 7 minutes or until golden.

3 Add the garlic and salt and sauté for 5 minutes.

4 Adjust the heat to high and add the mince. Cook for 15 minutes or until the liquid has evaporated. Use a wooden spoon to break down the mince into smaller pieces resembling crumbles.

5 Add the puréed tomatoes, tomato paste, sugar and pepper and bring to a simmer.

6 Reduce the heat to medium, add the herbs and cook for a further 10 minutes.

7 Toss the cooked spaghetti with the sauce so that the bolognaise emulsifies and thickens, and the sauce coats the pasta.

8 Serve in individual bowls and sprinkle with grated Parmesan and green chilli oil.

CARIEMA'S TIP

Don't discard the pasta water, you can add a ladle or two in step 7 to create a rich and velvety sauce.

REFRESHING LIQUID

VIRGIN SUNDOWNERS TO
QUENCH YOUR THIRST AND
REFRESH YOUR SOUL

Zest is defined as living life with a sense of exhilaration, anticipation and vigour! It is an essential element that nurtures our soul, uplifts our spirits and ultimately makes us human.

I read a beautiful quote by American author Karen Salmansohn that says: 'Cultivate the habit of zest. Purposefully seek out the beauty in the seemingly trivial. Especially in the trivial. The colours and shapes of the foods you eat. The shadows a vase makes on your table. The interesting faces of the people on the bus with you.' I've always been big on the small things in life, the grace that's required from me to truly appreciate the lessons life has to teach me. I can't say that I have always been welcoming of some of these lessons, but in hindsight, it's allowed me not to take anything for granted in my life.

My niece, Nabeelah, who resides in Dubai with me, reminds me of a younger version of me, a version filled with promise, excitement and purpose. It's only fitting that her energy permeates through this chapter of liquid nourishment. She's sassy, a go-getter, and no debate or conversation is mundane when she's around. Her representation of life's enjoyment is in the colourful, zesty and sweet drinks she mixes up for us! She loves creating mocktails, especially in a long-stem glass, with a rim encrusted with sugar or salt, and these often find their way into one of her cooling concoctions. For a refreshing tang, limes and lemons are added and as you can imagine, our pantry is often stocked with all sorts of cordials. True to her South African and Cape Malay roots, the only cordials she prefers to use is Rose's – the same brand my late father loved and her father adores.

In this chapter you get to sample the Isaacs' repertoire of virgin cocktails. Whether it's the blush of a mocktail named Afterglow or the tantalising tang of a Gourmet Margarita, one thing's for sure, our love language extends into liquid nourishment too.

May your thirst be quenched and your soul refreshed, with every sip!

Afterglow –
Orange, Pineapple and Granadilla

The first recipe in this chapter is one of the simplest because it has only four ingredients. It also allows me to utilise orange and pineapple juices, which we always have in our refrigerator at home. A dash of grenadine gives the Afterglow its blush.

SERVES 2 | **PREPARATION TIME** 10 minutes

1 C (250 ml) ice cubes
¼ C (60 ml) orange juice
¼ C (60 ml) pineapple juice
1 Tbsp (15 ml) grenadine cordial
Slices of pineapple or orange, for garnishing
Edible flowers, for garnishing

1 Half-fill two tumbler glasses with ice.
2 Divide the orange juice between the tumblers.
3 Divide the pineapple juice between the tumblers.
4 Tilt the tumbler sideways and slowly pour the grenadine down the side of the glass so that it sinks.
5 Give it a stir to create that 'blush' or leave it as is and garnish with a slice of orange and/or pineapple and edible flowers.

Piña Colada

You'll need to freeze the pineapple and coconut water cubes for this recipe, so it's best to do the prep the night before you'll be serving the piña coladas. The coconut milk and cream gives this mocktail its smooth and velvety texture and taste. This drink always makes me feel like I am on vacation and so the colourful cocktail umbrella is definitely needed for added bliss!

SERVES 2 | **PREPARATION TIME** 10 minutes

1½ C (325 ml) frozen pineapple chunks
1 C (250 ml) coconut water, poured into an
    ice-cube tray and frozen
1 can (400 ml) coconut milk
½ C (125 ml) coconut cream
½ C (125 ml) pineapple juice
Juice of 2 medium or 3 small limes
1 Tbsp (15 ml) honey, or to taste
Maraschino cherry syrup (optional)
Pineapple portions and maraschino or fresh
    cherries, for garnishing

1 Place the frozen pineapple chunks, coconut water ice cubes, coconut milk, coconut cream, pineapple juice and lime juice into a blender and blend until smooth.
2 Serve immediately, adding a swirl of maraschino syrup (if using) and a garnish of pineapple and cherries.

Uncle Joey's Cola Tonic

I have an uncle who could pretty much turn any drink, even tea, into a flavour explosion! Anything served at Uncle Joey (Yusuf) and Aunty Noori's (Nur) home was always elegant, classy and eccentric. Way back in the Eighties when Rose's lime cordial was all the rage, my Uncle Joey and my father really got into making drinks. My father loved the passion fruit concentrate and Uncle Joey's signature drink was this cola tonic, served in high-stem glasses, reminding us all just how fancy and free life could be.

SERVES 2 | **PREPARATION TIME** 5 minutes

2 shots (50 ml) Rose's Kola Tonic
    Flavoured Cordial
2 shots (50 ml) grapefruit juice
Ice cubes
Sprite or lemon-flavoured sparkling water,
    for topping up
Grapefruit peel and fresh mint leaves,
    for garnishing

1   Place the cola tonic, grapefruit juice and ice into a cocktail shaker and shake well.
2   Pour into ice-filled margarita glasses and top up with Sprite or the sparkling water.
3   Garnish with a curl of fresh grapefruit peel and a mint leaf.

Passion Fruit Mojito

I love the sweet, zesty and tangy taste of granadillas and the bright-yellow colour just reminds me of a beautiful sunny day. It is one of my favourite mojitos and it literally tastes like a vacation in a glass!

SERVES 2 | **PREPARATION TIM**e 10 minutes

2 C (500 ml) crushed ice

2 fresh granadillas, pips and juice or ¼ C (60 ml) granadilla pulp

¼ C (60 ml) Rose's Passion Fruit Flavoured Cordial

2 limes, quartered

⅓ C (80 ml) mint leaves, cut into chiffonade (roll into a cigar–shape and slice thinly)

2 C (500 ml) Sprite or lime- or lemon-flavoured sparkling water

2 sprigs fresh mint leaves, for garnishing

Slices of lime, for garnishing

1 Use 1 C (250 ml) of the crushed ice and divide this between two highball glasses. Set aside.

2 Place the fresh granadilla juice and pips (if you are using fresh fruit) or granadilla pulp and the passion fruit cordial into a jug.

3 Add the lime quarters, chopped mint leaves and the remaining crushed ice to the jug and use a long spoon or stirrer to mix.

4 Pour this over the crushed ice in the highball glasses.

5 Top up each glass with Sprite or sparkling water and garnish with a slice of lime and a sprig of mint.

Gourmet Margarita Mocktail

This tangy (and spicy) gourmet margarita is the perfect mocktail when you're chilling on a lazy Friday or Saturday afternoon and want to ease out of a chaotic work week. It's a frozen drink, sipped at leisure, not to be rushed. It requires you to be free, at peace and just living in the moment.

SERVES 2 | **PREPARATION TIME** 10 minutes | Overnight setting of ice cubes

2–4 ice-cube trays (depending on the size)
¼ C (60 ml) lime juice
¼ C (60 ml) grapefruit juice
¼ C (60 ml) orange juice
1 Tbsp (15 ml) honey or sugar, or to taste
1 Tbsp (15 ml) sea salt flakes, for the rim
1 tsp (5 ml) chilli powder, for the rim
Lime or lemon wedge, for the rim
1 C (250 ml) lime-flavoured sparkling water
Lime wedges or slices, for garnishing
Lemonade for topping up (optional)

1 Place the fruit juices and honey or sugar into a small jug and mix well. Do a taste test at this stage and adjust if needed.
2 Pour into ice-cube trays and allow to set overnight.
3 Place the salt flakes and chilli powder on a plate and give it a bit of a shake to mix together.
4 Glide the lime or lemon wedge around the rim of two margarita glasses. Immediately dip the rim of the glasses into the chilli salt. Set aside.
5 Place the prepared ice cubes and sparkling water into a blender and blend well.
6 Pour into the chilli-salt-rimmed margarita glasses and garnish with a wedge or slice of lime. Top up with lemonade, if desired.

CARIEMA'S TIP

You can use either freshly squeezed fruit or bottled juice for this drink.

Strawberry Mule
with Mint, Ginger and Lime

I love ginger – love it in food, love it pickled, love it as candy, love it in tea and certainly love it in drinks. The lime and ginger beer are perfectly balanced by the sweetness of the ripe, ruby-red strawberries.

SERVES 2 | **PREPARATION TIME** 15 minutes

8 strawberries, hulled and halved

6 sprigs fresh mint, cut into chiffonade (roll into a cigar-shape and slice thinly)

1 thumb-size piece fresh ginger, peeled and julienned

2 C (500 ml) crushed ice

½ C (125 ml) tonic water of choice

Juice of 1–2 limes

1 C (250 ml) ginger beer

Lime slices, wedges or quarters, for garnishing

2 whole strawberries, for garnishing

2 sprigs fresh mint, for garnishing

1 Place the strawberries, mint leaves and half of the julienned ginger into a mixing jug. Muddle with a wooden muddle pestle or the back of a wooden spoon until the strawberries are broken down into tiny pieces.

2 Add the ice, tonic water, lime juice and ginger beer. Stir to mix well.

3 Pour into enamel or copper mugs or whisky glasses and garnish with strawberries, mint leaves and the remaining julienned ginger. Serve immediately.

COMPLEMENTARY COMPANIONS

CONDIMENTS THAT MAKE EVERY MEAL BETTER

Condiments remain an essential part of the eating experience in many countries, and South Africa is no different. A side of tomato and onion relish, spicy chilli sauce, atchar, chakalaka or chutney is almost mandatory alongside a meal. For Cape Malays, condiments elevate and complement the accompanying dish. Furthermore, our love for condiments is inherent in the regions from where our forebears hailed. Sambals and blatjangs are representative of Indonesian and Malaysian cuisine, and accompany our traditional fare to this day.

The late Faldela Williams and Zainab Lagardien (my grandmother) remain iconic culinary figures in our Cape Malay history, along with the legendary Cass Abrahams. These doyennes represented an emergence of home cooks who told the Cape Malay story through their own experience of it. My grandmother and Faldela Williams, for instance, reminded us that much of the heart and soul of our gastronomic past was cultivated in a suburb called District Six. They both learnt the essential skills of preserving and pickling at an early age. Their tales, as well as those of so many of our mothers, grandmothers and great-grandmothers, echo of organic, farm-fresh ingredients that were always preferred.

I wanted this chapter to exude Cape Malay culinary legacy and to honour the women who have kept many of the older recipes alive. For this reason, Zahra Hendricks, who was born in Salt River, comes to mind. She reminisces about purchasing her favourite mango atchar for only 2 cents when she was a little girl. Over the years, she was able to study and live in Pakistan, where she had an opportunity to sample a variety of atchars. This influenced a heightened interest in making her own.

Back in Cape town, Zahra's mom, Gadija Williams, who was born in Loader Street, Bo-Kaap, is never too far away when atchars are made in their home kitchen. Zahra's jars of vegetable and fruit atchars can be found at farmers' markets, which is where I met her while desperately hoping to get my hands on her famous brinjal atchar.

What I adore most about Zahra is her unassuming notion of just how phenomenal she is. She's down to earth, has an infectious smile and a positive approach to life. Her mom, an English rose of note with her porcelain skin, rose blush cheeks and elegant demeanour, is as welcoming and hospitable as Zahra is.

Zahra's atchars can be eaten right out of the jar, with a spoon in hand, and you'll want nothing more. Though I might not have had an opportunity to walk away with her brinjal atchar, she's been kind enough to share the recipe with me. She cautioned me though, saying that she doesn't measure her ingredients – it's all down to your senses, i.e. the texture of the atchar when prepared and the amalgamation of spices, oils, and fruit or vegetables. She maintains that it's a sense she has when it is 'just right' – and as a Cape Malay home cook, I know exactly what she means!

Zahra's Zesty Brinjal Atchar

Zahra Hendricks's atchars are sought after in Cape Town's southern suburbs and though her range is extensive, she maintains that her brinjal atchar remains her personal favourite.

SERVES 6 × 375 ml jars | **PREPARATION TIME AND COOKING TIME** 40 minutes
PICKLING BRINJALS 3 hours | **DEHYDRATION TIME** 4 hours or **SHALLOW FRYING TIME** 40 minutes

FOR THE MASALA PICKLING LIQUID

10 cloves garlic, peeled
½ thumb-size piece fresh ginger, peeled
2 C (500 ml) white vinegar
30 whole dried red Kashmiri chillies
1 Tbsp (15 ml) turmeric
1 Tbsp (15 ml) cumin seeds
1 Tbsp (15 ml) black mustard seeds
1 C (250 ml) mustard oil or sunflower oil

FOR THE ATCHAR

10 large brinjals
3 Tbsp (45 ml) salt
½ C (125 ml) sunflower oil (optional)
2 Tbsp (30 ml) methi (fenugreek) or atchar masala
2 Tbsp (30 ml) dried chilli flakes
1 Tbsp (15 ml) ground cumin
1 Tbsp (15 ml) tamarind paste
2 C (500 ml) brown sugar

FOR THE TEMPERING SPICES

½ C (125 ml) sunflower oil
15 curry leaves
5 fresh green chillies, chopped
5 cloves garlic, peeled
3 whole dried red chillies
1 Tbsp (15 ml) black mustard seeds
½ tsp (2.5 ml) asafoetida

PREPARING THE MASALA PICKLING LIQUID

1. Place the cloves of garlic, ginger and vinegar into a food processor and pulse until it forms a smooth paste.
2. Add the Kashmiri chillies, turmeric, cumin and mustard seeds and pulse again until smooth. Set aside.
3. Heat the oil in a medium saucepan on medium heat, then fry the masala liquid for about 10 minutes or until the garlic and ginger are fragrant and cooked. Set aside.

PREPARING THE ATCHAR

1. Rinse and dry the brinjals thoroughly with a kitchen cloth or paper towel. Cut them into 2–3 cm cubes, sprinkle with the salt and leave for a minimum of 3 hours.
2. Rinse the brinjals, then drain in a colander. Squeeze out the excess water. Place the brinjal cubes on a wire rack and dry in the sun or shallow-fry in ½ C (125 ml) oil until crispy.
3. Add the methi or atchar masala, chilli flakes and cumin to the prepared masala pickling liquid. Fry for 10 minutes on medium heat, then add the tamarind paste and sugar and adjust the heat to low. Stir continuously for about 10 minutes until the sugar and tamarind have dissolved.
4. Add the dried or fried brinjal portions and mix thoroughly.
5. Add more vinegar or oil if you prefer a saucier consistency. Set aside.

THE TEMPERING PROCESS

1. Heat the oil in a small pan on medium to high heat. Add the curry leaves, green chillies, garlic cloves, red chillies, mustard seeds and asafoetida. Adjust the heat to medium and fry for about 7 minutes or until the garlic is golden. Remove the pan from the heat and add the tempered ingredients, including the oil, to the brinjal atchar.
2. Set aside to cool completely and then decant into sterilised jars. Serve immediately or store in the refrigerator for up to two months.

Tomato and Onion Relish
(Tamatie en Uiwe Slaai)

Tomato and onion relish is the crowning accompaniment in our Cape Malay culinary chest! So much so, that this relish was and still is served at weddings in Cape Town. It can be likened to the Indian onion and tomato relish that contains lemon juice instead of vinegar. My late grandmother in Bo-Kaap taught me how to make this relish. It contains only five ingredients, although these days fresh coriander is added and the brown vinegar is often substituted for white vinegar.

MAKES 2 × 375 ml jars | **PREPARATION TIME** 40 minutes, including resting time | **COOKING TIME** none

FOR PREPARING THE ONIONS

2 medium-size brown or white onions,
   thinly sliced
1 tsp (5 ml) salt
1 C (250 ml) boiling water

FOR THE RELISH

2 medium-size ripe tomatoes,
   finely chopped
1 fresh green chilli, thinly sliced
1 C (250 ml) brown or white vinegar
¼ C (60 ml) white or brown sugar
½ tsp (2.5 ml) salt

PREPARING THE ONIONS

1. Place the sliced onions into a bowl.
2. Add the salt and rub this into the onions.
3. Add the boiling water and set aside for 5–10 minutes.
4. Rinse under cool running water, then drain.

PREPARING THE RELISH

1. Place all the remaining relish ingredients into the same bowl as the onions.
2. Give everything a good stir and set aside for at least 20 minutes before serving.

CARIEMA'S TIP

Take time to prepare the onions as prescribed above, because it will mellow down their pungency and leave them tender and deliciously appetising. The relish can be stored in a glass jar in the refrigerator for up to two weeks.

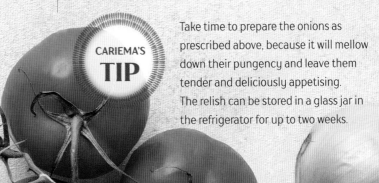

Roasted Beetroot and Onion Salad

Traditionally, my grandmother would boil the beets when preparing this salad. I've tweaked the recipe somewhat by roasting the beets and substituting the brown or white onions for red onions. Roasting allows the natural sugars of the beets to caramelise and complements the sweet red onions beautifully.

SERVES 6 | **PREPARATION TIME** 15 minutes | **COOKING TIME** 1 hour 45 minutes, including resting time

FOR THE VINAIGRETTE

¼ C (60 ml) extra virgin olive oil

⅓ C (80 ml) white vinegar

Salt to taste

½ tsp (2.5 ml) ground cumin

½ tsp (2.5 ml) freshly ground black pepper

FOR THE BEETROOT AND ONION SALAD

6 medium beetroots, rinsed and
  topped and tailed

2–3 Tbsp (30–45 ml) olive oil

1 medium red onion, peeled and
  thinly sliced

PREPARING THE VINAIGRETTE

1 Whisk all the ingredients together in a bowl. Set aside.

PREPARING THE BEETS

1 Preheat the oven to 200 °C.
2 Place the beetroots on a baking tray and drizzle with the olive oil.
3 Cover the baking tray with aluminium foil and roast for about 20 minutes.
4 Discard the foil and roast for a further 15 minutes or until the beetroots are tender.
5 Remove from the oven and allow to cool.
6 Peel off the skins and cut the beetroots into 2–3 cm cubes. Transfer to a mixing bowl.
7 Scatter the red onion slices over the cubed beetroots.
8 Pour the vinaigrette over the onions and beets and mix until everything is evenly coated with the vinaigrette.
9 Set aside for at least 1 hour at room temperature before serving.

Malaysian Chilli Paste

This chilli paste is an essential Malaysian condiment that is often also added to cooking. I use the long dried red chillies for this recipe because the smaller ones are blisteringly hot. If I am serving this as a condiment, I'd prefer that it complements the meal and does not overpower it with heat.

SERVES 4–6 | **PREPARATION TIME** 15 minutes, including resting time | **COOKING TIME** none

20 g (± 1 C [250 ml]) long dried red chillies
1 C (250 ml) boiling water

1 Place the chillies into a bowl and pour over the boiling water. Cover the bowl with plastic wrap and set aside for 10–15 minutes or until the chillies are tender and can easily be torn by hand.

2 Drain the chillies and transfer them to a food processer or blender.

3 Pulse until they form a smooth paste, adding a dash of water if needed.

4 Use immediately or store in a glass jar in the refrigerator for up to two weeks.

Copycat Green Chillies in Oil

Whenever I'm at an Ocean Basket restaurant, I can literally have this little condiment spread on bread. And when I'm at Tashas, it's the green chillies in olive oil sprinkled on my favourite chicken mayo sandwich, pasta or quesadillas that I love. I ended up making my own version, which now forms part of our ensemble of condiments in our refrigerator at home.

SERVES 4–6 | **PREPARATION TIME** 10 minutes | **COOKING TIME** none

20 g (± 1 C [250 ml]) long fresh green chillies
½ C (125 ml) olive oil

1 Place the chillies into a food processor or blender and pulse until it forms a coarse paste.

2 Transfer to a bowl and add the olive oil. Give it a good stir, then transfer to a clean jar and seal with a lid.

3 It can be stored at room temperature for about a week and for up to one month in the refrigerator.

Malaysian Chilli Sambal

This chilli sambal is traditionally made in Malaysia with shrimp or fish sauce, but I surmise that because these ingredients were not commonly consumed at the Cape of Good Hope at the time our forebears made their home here, the ingredients would have been omitted from the recipes that the Cape Malays had adopted. I also assume that fish sauce and shrimp paste would have been substituted with vinegar or tamarind. Cape Malays use granulated sugar to balance the acidity derived from the aforementioned ingredients, whereas Malaysians use jaggery, palm sugar or dark coconut sugar. I remember my Big Ma's love for substituting sugar with dark molasses, which can also be used for this recipe.

SERVES 4–6 | **PREPARATION TIME** 10 minutes | **COOKING TIME** 10 minutes

1 medium-size onion, roughly chopped

3 cloves garlic, peeled and crushed

½ thumb-size piece fresh ginger, peeled and roughly chopped

¼ C (60 ml) canola or sunflower oil

½ C (125 ml) chilli paste (page 191)

1 Tbsp (15 ml) tamarind paste or juice of ½ lemon

2½ Tbsp (37.5 ml) molasses or brown sugar

½ tsp (2.5 ml) salt

⅓ C (80 ml) water

1   Place the onion, garlic and ginger into a food processor or blender and pulse until it forms a smooth paste.

2   Heat the oil in a medium-size saucepan on medium heat.

3   Add the onion paste to the warm oil and allow to warm up for about 3 minutes.

4   Add the remaining sambal ingredients and adjust the heat to medium–high. Bring to a boil and then reduce the heat to low.

5   Simmer gently for 5–7 minutes.

6   Remove from the heat and allow to cool completely.

7   Use immediately or store in a glass jar in the refrigerator for up to two weeks.

Malaysian Sweet Chilli Sambal

This sambal is perfect as a dipping sauce for your favourite spring rolls, samoosas and pastries. I also add it when making fish cakes or frikkadel (meatballs), which not only makes them moist, but also adds depth of flavour.

SERVES 4–6 | **PREPARATION TIME** 10 minutes | **COOKING TIME** 10 minutes

4 cloves garlic, peeled and crushed

1 medium-size onion, roughly chopped

2 Tbsp (30 ml) canola or vegetable oil

2 Tbsp (30 ml) chilli paste (page 191) or 8 dried red chillies, soaked in boiling-hot water for 10 minutes, then drained and puréed

2 Tbsp (30 ml) sweet soy sauce

3 Tbsp (45 ml) molasses or brown sugar

1 Tbsp (15 ml) tamarind paste or lemon juice

1 tsp (5 ml) white vinegar

½ tsp (2.5 ml) salt

¾ C (200 ml) water

1. Place the garlic and chopped onion into a food processor or blender and pulse until it forms a smooth paste.
2. Heat the oil in a medium-size saucepan on medium heat.
3. Add the garlic and onion paste to the warm oil and allow to warm up for about 3 minutes.
4. Add the remaining sambal ingredients and adjust the heat to medium-high. Bring to a boil and then reduce the heat to low.
5. Simmer gently for 5–7 minutes.
6. Remove from the heat and allow to cool completely.
7. Use immediately or store in a glass jar in the refrigerator for up to two weeks.

Tomato and Onion Relish
(page 189)

Roast Beetroot
and Onion Salad
(page 190)

Zahra's Zesty
Brinjal Atchar
(page 188)

Copycat
Green Chillies in Oil
(page 191)

Malaysian
Sweet Chilli
Sambal
(page 193)

Malaysian Chilli Sambal
(page 193)

Malaysian Chilli Paste
(page 191)

Postscript

RASHIEDA ISAACS (1 August 1949–30 August 2021)

She comes to complete the circle...

I never knew just how much she completed the circle until I lost her in August 2021.

It's 5 a.m. in Dubai as I look out from my apartment building window onto the streetlights on Sheik Zayed Road below. I can't comprehend that another year is slowly coming to an end. I wish I could describe a lighter mood as I reflect on what 2021 has meant to me. This has clearly been a year of loss and reflection.

I remember, vividly, the words of my therapist as she described loss to me. She said: 'The mind, body and soul cannot distinguish the kind of loss it experiences – whether it's loss of a loved one through death, loss of a child as he or she heads off to university or leaves home, or loss of a lover who walks away, leaving you with only the pieces of your broken heart. The mind, body and soul only feel the emotions that encompass losing something that meant something to us. The body feels pain, the soul feels tormented, and the mind cannot find logic.'

This has been the year that I have come closer to death than I have ever been before, as I watched my mom take her last breath. I never appreciated how utterly comforting it was to hold her hand, the warmth of her palm in mine as I raised her hand to my lips and gently kissed her soft skin.

In retrospect, I could never have imagined how cold the human body becomes when death is the only thing that engulfs it. I could never have envisaged that my mom's lifeless body would be a reminder for me of just how vulnerable I am and how fragile we all are.

My need to control things in my life dissipated into thin air, as one last breath signified the end of a human life. This begs the question: how much control do we really ever have?

Death forces one to tie things up in one's life. To release what might have burdened us for many years. Death provides courage to the living and, almost in an instant, one seems bolder to set boundaries and then to communicate them with conviction. Death suddenly becomes a window to the past, reminding us to seize the moment. It whispers: *'Don't leave anything to tomorrow. Do it now!'* Death also has a way of lifting veils, allowing us to see things and people more clearly. It allows us to discard the masks we've worn for a long time and prompts us to show up in our most authentic form.

I cannot describe the months after her death as anything else but an internal struggle of my own belonging in this world. My purpose in balance and my zest for life were dampened by the age-old questions: *'Why am I here? What am I meant to do?'*

Since most of the trauma, heartache and pain I have ever felt came to me during my younger years, I was forced to revisit episodes in my life in order for me to heal again. The dark night of the soul had arrived – what was I to do with it?

No part of what I needed to revisit was easy. None of it came without deep regret and fear, anxiety and shame, disappointment and remorse. Some of the trauma had changed the course of my life, because of the choices I had made or the choices I had allowed others to make for me. It's fair to say that this past year has kicked me right in my gut and literally crippled me emotionally. There's a fitting quote by the Persian poet Rumi that says: 'When life pushes you down to your knees, you're in the perfect position to pray.' And so, I prayed...

I found peace in surrendering. I found solace in silence. I found me again in all of the pieces of my broken heart. I honoured the delicate space I found myself in and, over time, my body, soul and mind seemed to be in alignment again. It might have needed time, but I think this time around I felt compelled to pay full attention to what I needed in order to heal completely.

I remain curious about life and still believe that love in its purest form is my salvation.

Thus, just before dawn on a sombre Friday morning in Dubai, I found myself here – writing the manuscript to the book you hold in your hands and making a promise to myself to cook the way my mom would have wanted me to.

My culinary creed is more intense than before, as the translucent onions gently sizzling in glistening oil fill my kitchen with the aromas from my childhood. My domestic goddess persona is now amplified as I run my fingers along the fabric of beautifully crafted table linen, placing one pristine white porcelain plate on my table, then another and another. My smile is filled with gratitude as my guests pull up a chair, their eyes filled with glee, and their gracious gestures about the feast they see in front of them warms my beating heart. In that very moment, I vow to my mom that I will not enter into cooking, baking or eating with frivolity. I vow that my table will be a place where the coming together of souls is met and fed only with love!

I echo that the love language of the Cape Malays is food – long may this language be 'spoken' around the tables we sit at.

Mummy, this one's for you...

Gratitude

'IN GOD I MOVE AND BREATHE AND HAVE MY BEING'

I am ever grateful for the life that I have been granted, the people that I have met, the friends that have embraced me and the family that I was born into.

As I journeyed this world as a little girl, I had a vision of what my future could be like and my determination to bring it to life has been my saving grace. My story doesn't come without pain, it doesn't discount heartache and disappointment. It's been marred by ridicule and recklessness, tainted with a troubled view of what I should be versus what I could be. There are so many moments that were stolen, taken from me, so many lost and fleeting, and so many whispers that enticed me into the darkest of times. But just as darkness descends, light too will find its way back, slowly, gently and peacefully. Often during the moments of lightness, I feel the fullness of my life and I am eternally grateful.

After losing my mom, I developed a deeper appreciation for what it means to be a parent. It is certainly not for the fainthearted. Parenting demands, your time, your consciousness and your undivided attention. Whilst parenting, I have found myself revisiting my childhood years and focusing on the elements in my parents' home that made me feel grounded, that made me feel loved and safe.

I remembered my father's insistence to have all our meals at the table; we were never allowed to have meals in front of the TV or in separate rooms of the house. I fondly remembered his persistence of praying together, and often after prayers he'd speak to us about all religions. So as a child growing up in a Muslim home, I was already exposed to Judaism, Christianity and Hinduism in relation to world religions and how tolerant one should be of one another. Later, when I had questions about atheism and other alternate faiths, my father was the first person I would go to and this sparked off many of our visits to bookstores and libraries.

I started thinking about what made me feel safe and secure during different stages of growing up and, in that, discovered that maybe there may be elements that would be relevant, practical and pertinent in raising my own family. As a parent I also recognise that I am learning from my children, discovering the world through their eyes – a dynamic world that is changing at a rapid pace. A world very different to the one that I grew up in. I am even learning a new vocabulary with them; words such as gaslighting, throwing shade, ghosting, woke, etc.

I have also been exceptionally fortunate that I have a partner who takes to parenting like a fish to water! I think he was born to be a father. His calm and peaceful demeanour is the antidote to my anxiety and panic.

Our boys seem to mimic him and this is especially visible when I am ill. Turhaan will nudge me to get into a warm bath or shower, put on my PJs and tuck me into bed. He will then have a glass of water, my medication and a box of tissues on the bedside table. The curtain will be drawn slightly and I'll be asked if I am comfortable. If I hadn't eaten, he'll ensure that I have a bite to eat. My boys follow the same example when their dad is travelling or not home, they instinctively know what to do.

Similarly, my boys also notice when Turhaan and I swop roles when needed and that the relationship is a reciprocal one. Dr Shefali Tsabary, a clinical psychologist who wrote the book *The Conscious Parent*, says

that 'when you parent, it's crucial you realize you aren't raising a "mini me", but a spirit throbbing with its own signature.' This is the kind of parent I strive to be.

With every cookbook I write, I am deeply moved by the reflections that come to me during the entire process. I am especially thankful for being able to put words to my thoughts and to feel the emotions of the sentences as they become paragraphs and eventually tell a story.

I am thankful for many things in my life, but am most grateful to Turhaan, Tawfeeq and Tashreeq, who by all accounts have allowed me to live out my dreams! In pursuit of happiness, I have arrived here, with them at my side. They remain, always, the wind beneath my wings.

Glossary

Amasi – Sour milk, a popular South African yoghurt-like drink made from fermented milk.

Barakah – In Islam, 'barakah' or 'baraka' is the Arabic word for blessing. It implies that a blessing is a kind of continuity of spiritual presence and revelation that begins with God and flows through that and those closest to God.

Bird's-eye chillies – Also known as Thai chillies, these are used extensively in Asian dishes.

Bo-Kaap – A suburb close to the CBD of Cape Town, South Africa, also known as The Cape Malay Quarter. The cultural centre of Cape Malay heritage.

Braai – A South African term for barbecue, where meat and/or vegetables are grilled over an open fire.

Bredies – 'Bredie' is the Afrikaans word for stew, but is actually a word of Malaysian origin. This form of cooking was first introduced to the Cape by Malays, who were, in most cases, brought to the colony as slaves. Bredies generally are a spiced stew of mutton ribs, generally cooked with vegetables. In addition to tomato, they can also feature cauliflower, lentils, parsnips and quince, and are served with rice. Pumpkin, green beans and waterblommetjies (Cape water lily, *Aponogeton distachyos* flowers) are also used.

Brown vinegar – Brown spirit vinegar and brown grape vinegar are the most common vinegars available in standard supermarkets. Spirit vinegar is produced from the finest alcohol distilled from sugar cane. It is also an economical flavour enhancer when used in home cooking. Grape vinegar contains potassium and magnesium, and is an unrefined product, making it perfect as a standard cooking vinegar.

Boeta – 'Brother' is an informal or familiar title or term of address, but is also seen as addressing an uncle in Cape Malay communities and a show of respect when addressing a male elder or the eldest son.

Cape Malay Quarter – See Bo-Kaap.

Chiffonade – When leafy herbs or vegetables are rolled into a cigar shape and then cut very finely.

Crayfish – A freshwater crustacean resembling a small lobster.

Curry leaves – A shrub or small tree native to India and Sri Lanka, the aromatic leaves of which are widely used in Indian cooking. Buy fresh curry leaves that are still on their stem and have a deep green colour, which will provide robust flavour. Dried curry leaves keep well but are less flavourful than fresh ones. If using dried, remember to compensate for the loss of flavour by adding more leaves to your dish.

Curry powder – A blend of ground spices that come together to give a warm and earthy flavour to whatever dish in which it is used. Curry powders can vary in heat and are most commonly made up of dried and ground chillies, turmeric, cumin, cardamom, curry leaves and more.

Denningvleis – A hearty Cape Malay meat stew flavoured with bay leaves and tamarind or lemon juice. The word 'denning' originated from the Javanese 'dendeng', which referred to the meat of the water buffalo. Nowadays, however, cooks use mutton.

Eid al-Fitr – Literally means 'festival of the breaking of the fast' and is an important religious holiday celebrated by Muslims worldwide to mark the end of Ramadan, the Islamic holy month of fasting.

Eid al-Adha – Literally means 'festival of sacrifice'. It is the second of the two official holidays that are celebrated within Islam (the other being Eid al-Fitr). The day is also sometimes called Big Eid or the Greater Eid, or Labarang by Cape Malays.

Garlic and ginger paste – Puréed garlic cloves and fresh ginger mixed with oil.

Ginger – A subtropical plant that is grown for its knobbly root, which is used both fresh and dried as a seasoning. Though they can be used interchangeably, the flavour of fresh ginger is more pungent than dried, with heavy citrus, even acidic, notes.

Iftar – Iftar is the evening meal with which Muslims end their daily Ramadan fast at sunset. They break their fast at the time of the call for the evening prayer (adhan).

Julienne – A method of cutting vegetables into short, thin matchstick-like slices.

Komvandaan – Literally 'where we come from'. It is a colloquial term that describes the food and stories that have shaped the lives of so many people across communities in South Africa.

Mavrou – A Cape Malay traditional dish that is usually served at weddings, on Eid and other special occasions. Mavrou is a very colourful dish and is usually made with steak.

Rose water – Also sometimes spelled 'rosewater'. It is created by distilling rose petals with steam. Rose water has a very distinct and intense floral flavour and is often used in Middle Eastern, Persian and Indian cooking.

Smoor – The term 'smoor' is derived from the Indonesian word 'semur' and is connected to the Dutch word 'smoor', which means stewing or braising. A dish like 'semur daging' is a stewed beef dish with a heavy Dutch influence. However, Cape Malays refer to braised dishes as 'gesmoor' or 'gesmore' and then add the main ingredient to the second part of the word, for example gesmore steak.

Smoortjie – The diminutive form of smoor. It refers to a less expensive version of a traditional smoor. The base ingredients of a smoor or smoortjie are onions, tomato and garlic, with the possible addition of green chilli.

Slurry – A combination of starch (usually cornflour, flour, potato starch or arrowroot) and cold water, which is mixed together and used to thicken a soup, gravy or sauce.

Suhur – An Arabic word meaning 'of the dawn' or 'pre-dawn meal'. It refers to the meal consumed by Muslims before dawn before fasting begins during the Islamic month of Ramadan. The daily fast during Ramadan begins immediately after the pre-dawn meal of suhur and continues during the daylight hours, ending with sunset and the evening meal of iftar.

Tamarind paste – Originating from the tamarind tree indigenous to tropical Africa, which produces a pod-like fruit that contains a sweet, tangy pulp.

Thikr – Meaning 'remembrance', refers to Islamic devotional acts in which phrases or prayers are repeated.

Tietie – 'Sister' or 'Aunty' is an informal or familiar title or term of address, but is also seen as addressing an aunt in Cape Malay communities and a show of respect when addressing a female elder or elder sister.

Bibliography

BALJEKAR, M. (2019) *The Complete Indian Regional Cookbook*. Leicestershire: Lorenz Books, an imprint of Anness Publishing Ltd.

BAŞAN, G. AND BRIGDALE, M. (2009) *Vietnamese Food & Cooking*. London: Hermes House.

BHARADWAJ, M. (2016) *Indian Cookery Course*. London: Kyle Books, an imprint of Kyle Cathie Limited.

FORD, E. (2019) *Fire Islands: Recipes From Indonesia*. Sydney: Murdoch Books, an imprint of Allen & Unwin.

HAY, D., COURT, C. AND BUUREN, E. (2018) *Basics to Brilliance*. Houten: Spectrum.

ISAACS, C. (2016) *Cooking for My Father in My Cape Malay Kitchen*. Cape Town: Struik Lifestyle, an imprint of Penguin Random House South Africa.

ISAACS, C. (2019) *Spice Odyssey*. Cape Town: Struik Lifestyle, an imprint of Penguin Random House South Africa.

ISAACS, C. (2021) *Curried*. Cape Town: Struik Lifestyle, an imprint of Penguin Random House South Africa.

MUSA, N. (2016) *Amazing Malaysian*. London: Penguin Random House.

OLIVER, J., LOFTUS, D., BISS, L., STUART, P. AND VERITY, J. (2021) *Together*. Penguin Random House UK.

SIDERIS, N. (2015) *Tashas*. Johannesburg: Jonathan Ball.

WILLIAMS, F. (2012) *Cape Malay Illustrated Cookbook*. Cape Town: Struik Lifestyle, an imprint of Penguin Random House South Africa.

ZAHARA, R. AND LEONG, L. (2012) *Malay Heritage Cooking*. Singapore: Marshall Cavendish Cuisine.

Recipe Index